# UNDERSTANDING REVOLUTIONARY WAR AND INVALID PENSION LEDGERS 1818–1872 AND THE PENSION PAYMENT VOUCHERS THEY REPRESENT

Craig R. Scott, CG, FUGA

HERITAGE BOOKS
2014

# HERITAGE BOOKS

*AN IMPRINT OF HERITAGE BOOKS, INC.*

**Books, CDs, and more—Worldwide**

For our listing of thousands of titles see our website
at
www.HeritageBooks.com

Published 2014 by
HERITAGE BOOKS, INC.
Publishing Division
5810 Ruatan Street
Berwyn Heights, Md. 20740

Heritage Books by the author:

*Index to the Fairfax County, Virginia Register of Marriages, 1853–1933*
Constance K. Ring and Craig R. Scott

*The "Lost" Pensions: Settled Accounts of the Act of 6 April 1838, Revised Edition*

*New Jerusalem Lutheran Church Cemetery*
Marty Hiatt and Craig R. Scott

*Scott Family Finding Aids, Volume #1: Marriages, 1700–1900*

*Understanding Revolutionary War and Invalid Pension Ledgers, 1818–1872
and the Pension Payment Vouchers They Represent*

International Standard Book Numbers
Paperbound: 978-0-7884-5586-5
Clothbound: 978-0-7884-6019-7

Dedication

to

John Toler
Private
1$^{st}$ Virginia (Trueheart's) Regiment
War of 1812
who died in the War of 1812
and
Mary Parsons Toler Cameron
his widow
whose pension gave me fits.

# Table of Contents

# Introduction

The purpose of this pamphlet is two fold. First, to provide advice on how to be effective and efficient in pension ledger research. Second, a finding aid to pension ledgers and pension vouchers. These are Revolutionary War pensioners and some invalid pensioners of the War of 1812. A finding aid found in the Microfilm Reading Room of the National Archives, Washington, D.C. is the basis for this work. I also have many years experience with pension ledgers and payment vouchers.

This revised and expanded finding aid includes items missing from the original finding aid. It also includes ledgers missing from the original microfilming. There are few guidelines for pension voucher research. This work will detail the efficient steps necessary to use these records.

Most researchers do not realize that there is more to pension records than the pension application file. This is a mistake. There is the law that created the eligibility of the pensioner for the pension. No pensioner obtains a pension except by Congressional action and law. Knowing the Act can provide insight into the pensioner.

There is the application file with which most researchers are familiar. An application file envelope may contain more than one pension application file. When there is more than one pension in a single envelope, usually there will be the pension of the soldier and the pension of his widow. It is important to separate the applications by pensioner. Then arrange them in chronological order to understand the flow and voice of the pensioner.

Then there are the pension ledgers. Pension ledgers provide information that lead to information about our ancestors and their families. This information may not be in the application file. They will lead us to pension vouchers, last payment vouchers, and final payment vouchers. They also may tell us when pensioners move from place to place. Ledgers can provide clues to dates of death and the last payment vouchers might provide us the names of heirs. All in all, pension ledgers and payment vouchers have been a neglected genealogical source for many years.

These pension ledgers used to be available only on microfilm and were difficult to use without the finding aid. Today they are also available on Ancestry.com. With the ease of Ancestry.com, there is no excuse for not looking at the pension ledgers to see what they tell us about our ancestors. The recent addition of the *Index to Last and Final Pension Payments* on *Fold3.com* has improved our ability to locate the last and final payments. The last and final payments for Delaware and Georgia are on *Fold3.com*. As more and more state genealogical and historical societies are able to obtain funding or grants to digitize these records, they will become more accessible to researchers.

The finding aid to many of the missing last and final payments, *The Lost Pensions: Settled Accounts of 6 April 1838, Revised Edition,* may assist in the finding of missing payments from the last and final payment series.

Considering the now ready access to the pension ledgers and the index to last and final payments, this might seem like the inappropriate time to publish a finding aid to these records. Having access to records is one thing. Knowing how to use them is another. The purpose of this finding aid is to help you to understand the kinds of information in these records. What you get from the full use of these records. With the easy availability of these records you must consult them for each pensioner as part of a reasonable exhaustive search.


Craig R. Scott, CG, FUGA
1 July 2014

# Pension Ledgers

The pensions that are the focus of this pamphlet are the various Revolutionary War and Old Wars pensions paid under various acts from the end of the Revolutionary War until the last act dealing with Revolutionary War widows in 1858. They include Revolutionary War survivor pensions awarded under the Acts of 1818, 1820, 1826, 1828 and 1832. They include Revolutionary War widow pensions paid under the acts of 1836, 1838, 1843, 1844, 1848, 1853 and 1858. They include payments made to invalid pensioners paid under the Old Wars pension act. Some widows of soldiers who died in the War of 1812 are in these ledgers, if paid before 1873.

The records of pension payments are in the National Archives among the records of the Accounting Officers of the Department of the Treasury, Record Group 217. The payment ledgers, which reflect the regular semi-annual payments to pensioners. They may or may not provide information not found in pension application files. They will always provide information about the date or quarter and the pension agency at the time of payment.

A pensioner was due a payment for a pension during March and September of each year. The pensioner or a representative with power of attorney in hand would present himself or herself to the pension agent to get the payment. The pension agent was usually located in a bank. The government appointed pension agents in areas where there were enough pensioners to warrant opening a pension office. When the number of pensioners declined, the government would close the pension office.

The pension agent would pay the amount due. This would result in the creation of a receipt signed by the pensioner or the representative. The pension agent would keep a copy. The pensioner or his representative would also get a copy.

Pension agents would forward a "Quarterly Abstract of Payments" with supporting documentation to Washington, D.C. The pension payment vouchers were the supporting documentation. An Auditor in the Department of the Treasury would record the information in a ledger. The papers were then filed by pension agency, quarter of payment, and by the pension act.

The original ledgers are on microfilm. That microfilm is T-718, Ledgers of Payments, 1818-72, to U.S. Pensioners Under Acts of 1818 through 1858, From the Records of the Office of the Third Auditor of the Treasury. There are 23 rolls of microfilm. Digitized images are available as "U.S. Pensioners, 1818 – 1872" on Ancestry.com. This series of records is the primary source for information relating to the locations of payment vouchers. The arrangement of the ledgers is by pension act and then by pension agency.

What follows on the next page is a sample of a pension ledger page taken from the microfilm.

Note that this page is from the Massachusetts Pension Agency and that the ledger tracks with payments made under the Act of 1832. This act creates eligibility for pensions to militiamen who served at least six months during the Revolutionary War. Some Continental soldiers who were not eligible under the Act of 1818 became entitled by this act. The Act of 1832 made payments retroactive to March 1831.

The Header.

The top of the header is the name of the pension agency. Sometimes it is the name of a city and state. Many times; just the state. The ledger shown below begins in March 1831. It is the first ledger created under the Act of 1832 for this agency. In 1850 they made a new ledger to cover the payments made after 1850. You may have to look at more than one ledger to learn of the full history of a pensioner's payments.

The names on this page begin with the letter "K". It is normal for the ledgers are in alphabetical order by first letter of surname.

This first part of the ledger is the header. The meaning is fairly clear at this point. The "K" means the letter "K" and nothing more. The "6" means that the value in this column represents a six month value. Normally, it is just a single months value. The value of the allowance is usually a function of the rank of the individual at the time of his discharge from military service.

| NAME. | RANK. | *6.* Monthly Allowance. | COMMENCEMENT. |
|---|---|---|---|
| *h:* | | | |

Payments could be made by March and September of each year. Pensioners would often obtain their payments long after they were eligible to do so.

*Massachusetts.*

| 1831 | | 1832 | | 1833 | | 1834 | | 1835 | | 1836 | | 1837 | | 1838 | | 1839 | | 1840 | |
|---|---|---|---|---|---|---|---|---|---|---|---|---|---|---|---|---|---|---|---|
| March. | September. | March. | September. | March. | September. | March. | September. | March. | September. | March. | September. | March. | September. | March. | September. | March. | September. | March. | September. |

The entry part of the ledger of looks like this:

This is a larger view of the name side of the ledger:

| Name | | Rank | Payment |
|---|---|---|---|
| *Isaac* | *Kingman* | | *14.78* |

The entry side is a little more complicated.

3

Note that the only large numbers are 1, 2, 3, and 4. These represent the quarter the payment was gvien. Payments were usually made in the first and third quarters.

| S | M | S | M | S | M | S | M | S | M | S | M | S | M | S | M | S |
|---|---|---|---|---|---|---|---|---|---|---|---|---|---|---|---|---|

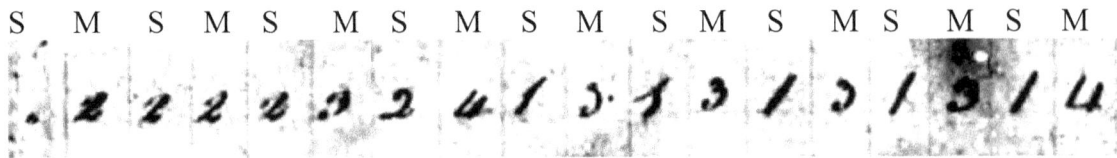

1 = 1<sup>st</sup> Quarter: January, February, March

$1 = 1^{st}$ Quarter: January, February, March

$2 = 2^{nd}$ Quarter: April, May, June

$3 = 3^{rd}$ Quarter: July, August, September

$4 = 4^{th}$ Quarter: October, November, December

Sometimes, when a pension payment was picked up later than March or September and into the next year, there is a notation of the payment year before the quarter mark.

It may look like $^{34}1$ or $^{34}2$ or $^{34}3$ or $^{34}4$.

The notation 341 can only occur in a period before 1834.

This notation if found in the September 1833 column means that the September 1833 payment was in the first quarter of 1834.

We can learn from these entries whether, that if a pensioner moved during the period of his pension payments. It is possible that he moved, but did not move far enough to warrant transferring to a different pension agency.

The final part of the ledger is the remarks made after the last notation. Sometimes there is information about the pensioner in the tail of the entries. It may say that the pensioner transferred to another pension office. It may say when the pensioner died, the date of the final payment. In the case of a last payment it might include the name of the new pension agency if the pensioner moved..

Died 11 Nov 1839               Paid  Date

In the case of this pensioner the last payment to the pensioner (or the representative) was in the 4th Quarter of 1839. The ledger states that Kingman died on 11th Nov. 1839. It also notes that the final payment in the 1st Quarter of 1840. By definition that is a payment to the heirs of the pensioner (under the applicable state law at the time of payment).

If there is no information in this remarks area it is likely that the last payment in the ledger is the last payment. A last payment may occur in 1820 because a pensioner receiving payments under the Act of 1818 was unable to prove that he was poor enough to continue his pension under the Act of 1820.

If there is information in the remarks area relating to a date of death it is likely that the last notation is a final payment. That last payment voucher might contain information about heirs.

# Pension Payments

## Pension Payment Vouchers

A pension payment voucher is the proof of payment. A pension agent paying either a pensioner or to the legal representative of the pensioner. Pension vouchers account for the disbursement of federal funds under one of the various pension acts of the Congress.

The pension agent was the representative of the government in the pension payment process. The government provides appropriated funds to the pension agent who has responsibility for safeguarding government funds and ensuring their proper disbursement to pensioners according to applicable law.

A pensioner would appear at the pension office with his pension certificate or his representative with a power of attorney and a facsimile of that certificate, endorsed by a county or local court official.

The pension payment vouchers are in the National Archives, Washington, D.C. These pension payment vouchers in this series of ledgers are in Record Group 217, Records of the Accounting Officers of the Department of the Treasury, Entry 721, Settled Accounts of Pension Agents, January 1813 – June 1899. They are in alphabetical order by name of state, and then by location of the pension agency, and then by type of pension and then by first letter of surname.

Few researchers have examined pension payment vouchers, other than the last and final payments. Most often because they were in the National Archives in College Park, Md. before 2008. Their transfer to the Washington, D.C. facility was a boon to all military pension researchers, not just those interested in the Revolutionary War.

The information in these payment vouchers varies. At a minimum they contain information on the location of a  pensioner in a particular time and place.

## Last payments

Although the schedule of periodic payments may not be rich in genealogical information the last payment may help to pinpoint the date of death. To receive each payment the pensioner would sign his or her name, or make a mark before witnesses, or give an individual a power of attorney. Each payment required either a mark or signature. In the absence of information to the contrary, you can determine a approximate date of death. Base the calculation on the periodic nature of the pension payment process. Semi-annual pension payment dates were 4 March and 4 September of each year. If the last payment was in September 1838 the next payment would be due on 4 March 1839. If the pensioner did not claim the March 1939 payment, one could hypothesized that he died between 3 September 1838 and 4 March 1839. This determination is possible in the absence of information in other records to the contrary and knowing that it is just a probable conclusion.

A missing payment might reflect the pensioner's move to another pension agency. Most times a transfer to another pension agency is noted, but not always. So exercise care must in a death calculation.

## Final Payments

Final payments reflect payments made to heirs or their representative after the death of the pensioner. The easiest way to determine if there is a final payment is to consult the series of records found on Fold3.com known as "Index to Final Pension Payments." The presence of an asterisk in the record indicates that a final payment has been located. Entries in the pension ledger, which are final payments are usually identified by the notation of the pensioners date of death and the date (quarter and year) of the final payment.

Final payments are the richest records, genealogically speaking. They can provide date and place of death, widow's name, names of children (usually under the age of sixteen) and sometimes the married names of daughters, and of sons and daughters-in-law, and addresses. The names of witnesses on the documents are often either relatives or close associates of the pensioner's family. Names and dates of death of deceased heirs and of their heirs are sometimes identified. On rare occasions it includes the date and place of the pensioner's burial.

## Published Last and Final Pension Payment Abstracts

Published abstracts about last and final pensions:

Kathryn McPherson Gunning, *Selected Final Pension Payment Vouchers, 1818–1864, Pennsylvania: Philadelphia & Pittsburgh* (Westminster, MD: Willow Bend Books, 2003)

Kathryn McPherson Gunning, *Selected Final Pension Payment Vouchers, 1818–1864, Rhode Island* (Westminster, MD: Willow Bend Books, 1999).

Alycon Trubey Pierce, *Selected Final Pension Payment Vouchers, 1818–1864, Alabama: Decatur, Huntsville, Mobile, Tuscaloosa* (Lovettsville, VA: Willow Bend Books, 1997)

Alycon Trubey Pierce, *Selected Final Pension Payment Vouchers, 1818–1864, District of Columbia* (Leesburg, VA: Willow Bend Books, 1998)

Alycon Trubey Pierce, *Selected Final Pension Payment Vouchers, 1818–1864, Louisiana: New Orleans* (Athens, GA: Iberian Publishing, 1996)

Alycon Trubey Pierce, *Selected Final Pension Payment Vouchers, 1818–1864, Maryland: Baltimore* (Lovettsville, VA: Willow Bend Books, 1997)

Alycon Trubey Pierce, *Selected Final Pension Payment Vouchers, 1818–1864, Mississippi:* Natchez and Jackson (Athens, GA: Iberian Publishing Co., 1997)

Alycon Trubey Pierce, *Selected Final Pension Payment Vouchers, 1818–1864, New Jersey: Trenton*, 2 vols. (Westminster, MD: Willow Bend Books, 2000)

Alycon Trubey Pierce, *Selected Final Pension Payment Vouchers, 1818–1864, South Carolina: Charleston* (Athens, GA: Iberian Publishing Co., 1997))

Settled Accounts under the Act of 16 April 1838

Some payments were not processed according to the normal process and are not part of the series of payment vouchers, last payments and final payments described above.

***The "Lost" Pensions: Settled Accounts of the Act of 6 April 1838*** is a finding aid to payment records found in the series of records entitled "Settled Accounts for Payment of the Accrued Pensions (Final Payments)." They are found in the National Archives in Entry 724, Records of the Third Auditor, Records of the Accounting Officers of the Department of the Treasury, Record Group 217. They represent accounts from the Revolutionary War, War of 1812, various Indian Wars before 1860, and the Mexican War. Many of the individuals identified in this list are not found in the pension indexes familiar to genealogists that cover the periods of those wars.

There are two editions. The first in 1997. A revised 2013 edition took into account the flat filing and preservation of the material which occurred following the publication of the first edition.

The records are by year and then by account number. They are settled accounts for pensions claimed under the various acts prior to and including the provisions of the U.S. Congressional Act of April 6, 1838. This act permitted persons to claim from the Treasury of the United States payments that had accrued to the pensioner and had not been claimed in pension offices for over eight months. Under this act funds remaining in pension offices after eight months were returned to the Treasury.

This explains why they are found in a separate series. Normally we would expect to find pension payment vouchers in RG 217, either Entry 721 (for pension vouchers) or Entry 722 (last and final payments).

The accounts frequently show the pensioner's date and place of death and the names of heirs. They may include supporting documentation, such as proof of identity of the claimant, pension certificates, powers of attorney, and related correspondence. In some cases, where the payment was the result of Congressional action a copy of the bill is included in the payment file. Other types of claims found in files include claims of special contractors for rations and forage. Not all of the records identified in the "Lost Pensions" book are final payments. Some are five-year half pay pensions. Widows of soldiers who died in the War of 1812, Indian Wars, and the Mexican War were entitled to payments every six months at half-pay, for a period of five years, if they did not remarry. Orphans under the age of sixteen collected if their mother remarried.

# Searching for a Payment Record

There are two procedures for searching for a record. You may use subscription databases or view the microfilm copies of the ledgers.

Manual procedure

1. Obtain a copy of the pension application file from either Fold3.com or the pension application file microfilm and abstract the following information:

   Pensioner's name (as it appears in the pension application file)
   Pension Certificate Number
   Amount of the pension payment
   Date of the act under which the payments were made
   Pension agency name

   [This information can be found on the tri-fold record found in each file. There may be more than one of these tri-folds and each should be examined for this information. Look for any pension increases indicated on this document, which is actually the original pension jacket.]

2. Examine the index to the register of pension payments found in Appendix B. The register is arranged by State in which the pension agency was located, and then by the name of the city where the pension office was located. Abstract from the register the volume and page numbers relating to all payments made by that agency for the act under which the pension payments were being made.

3. Examine the various ledgers on NARA microfilm publication, T718, Pension Ledgers. There will be a number (1, 2, 3, or 4) under each year in which a payment was made. These represent the quarter in which the payment was made.

   > Quarter 1 = January, February, March
   > Quarter 2 = April, May, June
   > Quarter 3 = July, August, September
   > Quarter 4 = October, November, December

When the last entry for the pensioner is followed by a date of death, and other information; you have found a final pension payment.

If the date of death is not entered in the register following the last payment notation, then the pensioner's date of death or the names of his heirs are unlikely to be found in the pension payment voucher.

Regardless, if the date of death appears in the ledger copy down the following:

Date of Last Payment (e.g.., 1839 – 3<sup>rd</sup> Quarter)
Date of Death
Any notations following the date of death
The volume and page number containing the information above.

Fill out a request form and order the pension payment voucher.

## Using for fee subscription services

This methodology requires a subscription to *Ancestry.com* and *Fold3.com* (optional for a step)

Three types of records are available online at this point and time.

1) the pension ledgers on *Ancestry.com*

2) the Index to Final Pension Payments on *Fold3.com*

3) Selected states Last and Final Payments available on *Fold3.com*

## The Pension ledgers on *Ancestry.com*

The most efficient method for finding an individual in the pension ledger on Ancestry is to use the SEARCH tab and access the CARD CATALOG. In the search screen for the CARD CATALOG type the word "Pensioners" in the TITLE box. The database that needs to be searched is U.S. Pensioners, 1818 – 1872. Click on that choice to go to the search screen for that database. Enter the name of the person of interest and ther result will lead you to the appropriate pension ledgers page.

## Index to Final Pension Payments on *Fold3.com*

The most efficient method for finding an individual in the index to last and final payments is to use the "Final Payments Vouchers Index for Military Pensions, 1818 – 1864" images. It can be most easily found by using the SEARCH tab and LIST ALL RECORDS. In the RECORDS ON FOLD3 search box type "Final". This will list the Final Payment Vouchers databases on Fold3. Select the "Final Payment Vouchers Index for Military Pensions, 1818 – 1864." In the search box type the name of the person that is of interest. This will take you to a screen that should mention your person.

## Selected States Last and Final Payments.

Using the procedure for searching the "Index to Final Pension Payments" above except substitute the "Final Payment Vouchers" images and continue.

At the time of this publication the Final Pension Payments were available on Fold3 for Delaware and Georgia. They are also available on NARA microfilm.

M2079, *Final Revolutionary War Pension Payment Vouchers: Delaware, 1997*

M1746, *Final Revolutionary War Pension Payment Vouchers: Georgia, 1993*

Case Study #1: The death of Isaac Kingman

Isaac Kingman was a soldier living in Massachusetts during the Revolutionary War. Usually the first record searched for information on a Revolutionary War soldier is his pension file or the pension file of his widow. Not all Revolutionary War soldiers will have pensions, usually because they did not live long enough to qualify under the law extant prior to their death or because they had insufficient qualifying service or were unable to prove that service. Not all soldiers have Compiled Military Service Records (CMSR). Isaac Kingman is an example of a soldier who received a pension, but does not have a CMSR. Isaac Kingman's wife, Content Kingman did not apply for a pension. We are able to determine that she did not apply for a pension because her name is not on the pension jacket. Had she done so the pension number (S18917) would have been either a number beginning with the letter "W" if she had been successful in obtaining a pension based on the service of Isaac Kingman, or an "R" if she had been rejected. At this point in the research we do not know if she predeceased Isaac.

The pension jacket tells us that Isaac Kingman served from Massachusetts. We know that he was successful in obtaining a pension because of the letter "S". The pension certificate issued was numbered 18917.

Here is a copy of the pension jacket found on www.Fold3.com:

When you look in the pension file of Isaac Kingman you find the original tri-fold pension jacket. There are several useful pieces of information..

First is the notation of "d. Nov. 11, 1839". This is his date of death. However, it is not proof of his date of death. It is a notation made by a pension clerk.

There is no further information in the pension that supports this date as his date of death.

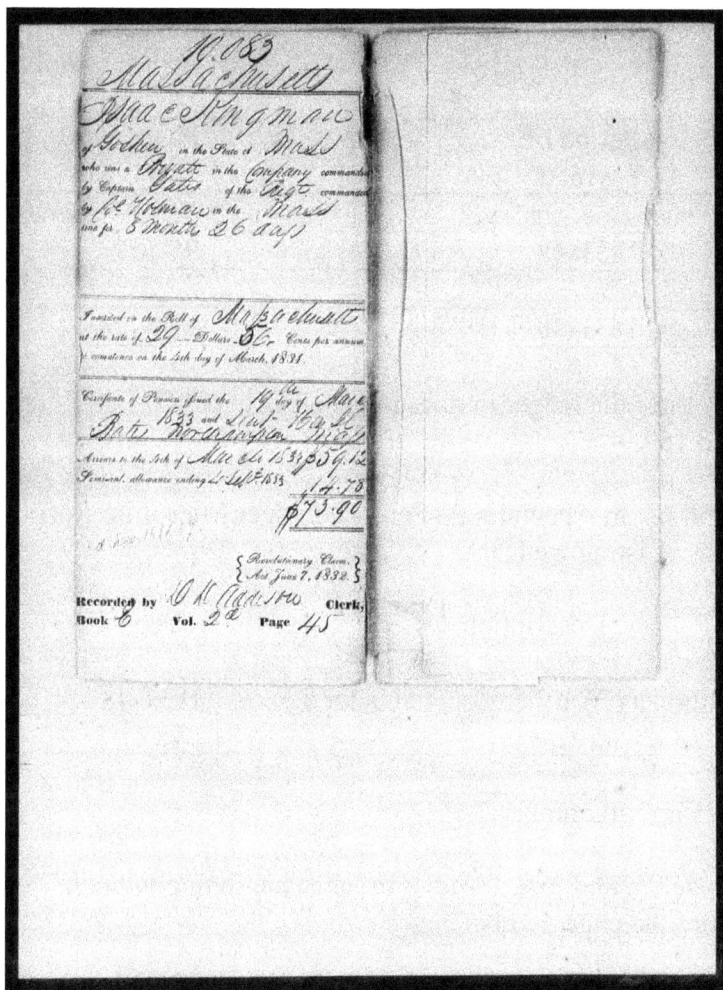

But there is information that is helpful. From this pension jacket we learn that Kingman is being paid by the Massachusetts Pension Agency under the Act of 4 June 1831. This means that he pension began in March 1832 with the first payment being retroactive to 4 June 1831.

If we are using the microfilmed records, and not *Ancestry.com*, then we would find the Massachusetts entries for the Act of 1832 and look for the Isaac Kingman entry.

In the absence of an online source for the Massachusetts pension ledgers this is the information necessary to start your search.

Act of 1832

Massachusetts

Payments beginning in 1832.

In the case of Isaac Kingman this is the entry that we are looking for. There are two entries in the chart in the Appendix B, Pension Office Listing, for Massachusetts, that match this criteria.

| Agency | Location | Act or Acts | Period of Payment | Volume | Pages |
|--------|----------|-------------|-------------------|--------|-------|
|        |          | 1832        | 1831-48           | G      | 95-159 |
|        |          | 1832        | 1831-48           | J      | 274-278 |

The first place that we want to look for the ledger in question is on Ledger "G" somewhere between pages 95 and 159.

By consulting the microfilm roll list in Appendix A, Pension Ledger Microfilm Roll Listing we learn:

| Roll | Volume | | Description | Years |
|------|--------|--|-------------|-------|
| 7 | G | | Revolutionary War Pensioners Under the Act of 1832 | 1831-48 |

So Ledger "G" is on T719, microfilm roll number 7.

We would begin our search on page 95, and look for the surnames beginning with "K" which we find on page 127. Record the page number.

Note that this page is from the Massachusetts Pension Agency and that the ledger begins in March of 1832. All of the names on this page deal with the letter "K". The ledgers are generally in alphabetical order by first letter of surname.

Lets look at the pieces of a pension ledger page.

At the top is the name of the pension agency. This ledger begins in 1831 and is the first ledger created for the Act of 1832 for this agency. The next ledger begins in 1852. Sometimes you might have to look at the first and second ledgers for a pension agency location when dealing with the Act of 1818 or 1832.

| NAME. | RANK. | Monthly Allowance. | COMMENCEMENT. |
|---|---|---|---|
| k. | | | |

Payments would be made in March and September of each year. The pensioner or a person holding the power of attorney of the pensioner would pick up the payment from the pension agency. Usually the pension agency was located in a specified bank and a banker was the pension agent.

*Massachusetts.*

| 1831 | | 1832 | | 1833 | | 1834 | | 1835 | | 1836 | | 1837 | | 1838 | | 1839 | | 1840 | |
|---|---|---|---|---|---|---|---|---|---|---|---|---|---|---|---|---|---|---|---|
| March. | September. | March. | September. | March. | September. | March. | September. | March. | September. | March. | September. | March. | September. | March. | September. | March. | September. | March. | September. |

The ledger part of Isaac Kingman is three names from the bottom of the page and looks like this:

This is a larger view of the name side of the ledger:

| Name | Rank | Payment |
|---|---|---|
| Isaac Kingman | | 14 78 |

Note that the only large numbers are 1, 2, 3, and 4. These represent the quarter the payment was made in.

16

$1 = 1^{st}$ Quarter: January, February, March

$2 = 2^{nd}$ Quarter: April, May, June

$3 = 3^{rd}$ Quarter: July, August, September

$4 = 4^{th}$ Quarter: October, November, December

Died 11 Nov 1839          Paid  Date

In the case of Isaac Kingman the last payment was made to him personally in the 4th Quarter of 1839. There is a notation that he died on $11^{th}$ Nov. 1839. We can see that the final payment was made in the $1^{st}$ Quarter of 1840.

This is the second place that mentions the death of Isaac Kingman. This date matches the date found on the original pension jacket. However, there is no indication of the source for this information.

*Fold3.com* can be checked for last or final payment card. Since the information on the card (actually it is a slip of paper, not a card) came from the pension ledger microfilm it will should match. The card may show an asterisk (*) in the upper left-hand corner. An asterisk means the last or final payment voucher was removed from the collection of pension payment vouchers and are now found in RG 217, Entry 722 insteadn of Entry 721 An asterisk means that a last or final payment was found when this series of Last and Final payments was created. These records are kept at Archives One in Washington, D.C.

This index card was found on Fold3.

| NAME | Kingman, Isaac |
| --- | --- |
| AGENCY OF PAYMENT | MASS |
| DATE OF ACT | 1832 |
| DATE OF PAYMENT | 1 qr 1840 |
| DATE OF DEATH | Nov 11, 1839 |

**FINAL PAYMENT VOUCHER RECEIVED FROM THE GENERAL ACCOUNTING OFFICE**

GENERAL SERVICES ADMINISTRATION     GSA DC 70-7035     FORM GSA DEC 69 **7068**

There was a Final Payment - a payment made after the death of the pensioner. The First Quarter, 1840 is after the date of death, November 11, 1839. There is likely to be some interesting genealogical information in the final payment voucher file.

A Last or Final Payment is obtained

X
X
X
X
X
X
X

Pulling the Final Payment File of Isaac Kingman at the National Archives, Washington, D.C. we find the following.

Kingman, Isaac

Mass

1832

This is the tri-fold envelope that contains the final payment. It provides the name of the pensioner (Isaac Kingman), the pension agency (Massachusetts), and the date of the Act of the pension (1832).

This is the application for the pension payment. Write down the names of all the persons found in the payment file. Each of these individuals might have some relationships to the person receiving the final payment. From this record we also learn that Cornelia Kingman is the wife of Isaac Kingman and that she is the widow of Isaac Kingman. One of the reasons that needs to be examined is her date of death. It might be before 1836 when she would have been eligible for a pension. She was eligible for a pension in 18136 because she married Isaac Kingman in 1769, which was prior to the expiration of this enlistment. Betsy Kingman is the daughter of Isaac Kingman and Content Packard Kingman.

# REVOLUTIONARY PENSIONERS.

### Under the Act of June 7, 1832.

No. _____ **OFFICE OF DISCOUNT AND DEPOSIT OF**

The Bank ~~of the United States~~ at Boston, _June 2_ 183_6_

RECEIVED of the PRESIDENT, Agent for paying Pensioners,
belonging to the State of *Massachusetts,*

_Five_ **Dollars,** _57_ **Cents,**

being for _four months & 7 days_ ~~**Months'**~~
Pension due to _Isaac Kingman dec_.

From the 4th day of _Septr_ 183_8_
to the 4th day of _November Seven_ 183_9_

for which I have signed Duplicate Receipts.

$5 57

_Joseph Orcutt_

This is the receipt that was forwarded by the pension agent to Washington to account for the disbursement of the funds from the Massachusetts pension agency. A similar receipt was provided to Joseph Orcutt to take back to Content Kingman to account for the pension payment.

This is the proof of the death of Isaac Kingman. I document signed by a Clerk of Court that attests to the death of Isaac Kingman. This is the final document in our journey through the pension application file, the pension ledger, and the final payment to establish the date of death of Isaac Kingman.

The purpose of this first case study was to acquaint you with pension ledgers using the microfilm.

In the next case study we will focus on how to use online subscription services to get to the information.

Case Study #2 – Daniel Waldo, one of the last surviving soldiers of the Revolution

Hillard referred to Daniel Waldo as "the most widely known of the surviving soldiers of the Revolution." Hillard arrived at his house after his death, but included a biography of him in *Last Men of the Revolution*. Born in Windham, Connecticut he was drafted as a soldier at sixteen for one month of service and later enlisted for an additional term. According to his pension application he was taken prisoner in December 1779 and released in February 1780 from the famous Sugar House Prisons in New York known for their cruel treatment of inmates. After the War he became a Congregational minister, married and had several children. There are several different CDV's of Waldo from the 1860s. One of them is found on the front cover of this pamphlet.

This is the original pension jacket.

Waldo, Daniel
Albany, NY
1832

This is the tri-fold envelope that tells us that Daniel Waldo is being served by the Albany Pension Office and has obtained a pension under the Act of 1832.

APPLICATION FOR A TRANSFER.

State of New York, }
County of Onondaga } ss.

On this 8th day of June 18[illegible]2

before me, the subscriber, a Justice of the Peace for the said County of Onondaga personally appeared [illegible] who, on his oath, declares that he is the same person who formerly belonged to the Company commanded by Captain Wales in the Regiment commanded by Colonel [illegible] in the service of the United States; that his name was placed on the pension roll of the State of Connecticut from whence he has lately removed; that he now resides in the State (District, or Territory,) of New York where he intends to remain, and wishes his pension to be there payable, in future. The following are his reasons for removing from the State of Connecticut to the State of New York. This deponent is now & has been for the last [illegible] years [illegible] from the state of Connecticut to Wayne County in the State of New York to preach to a congregation in Kent County in the year 1835 [illegible]

Sworn and subscribed to before me, the day and year above written. [illegible]

David Wales

[illegible]

(over)

When a pensioner would move he would transfer from one pension office to another. Usually this would be accomplished by the form above.

Here is where we learn of the heirs of Daniel Waldo.

Don't forget to look at the pension ledger.

34th CONGRESS, 1st Session

# H. R. 468.

[In concurrence]

IN THE HOUSE OF REPRESENTATIVES

June 20, 1856

Read twice, and committed to a Committee of the Whole House.

Mr. Bacon, from the Committee on Revolutionary Pensions, reported the following bill:

## A BILL Act 5

Providing an increase of pension to Daniel Waldo, of Onondaga county, New York.

Be it enacted by the Senate and House of Representatives of the United States of America in Congress assembled, That the Secretary of the Interior cause the pension of Daniel Waldo, of Onondaga county, New York, to be changed on the pension roll from twenty-six dollars and sixty-six cents per annum, to eight dollars per month, commencing from the fourth of March, eighteen hundred and thirty-one, and to continue during his natural life.

Approved Aug. 23, 1856

Dept of State
Aug 30, 1856

A true copy compared with the original bill

[signature] Carter
Chief Clerk

A bill to increase the pension of Daniel Waldo.

Case Study #3:

Hedgeman Triplett
S11575

SERVICE Va.

Triplett, Hedgeman

NUMBER S. 11.572

CONTENTS

This is the pension envelope found on Fold3.

According to his pension Hedgeman Triplett enlisted 1775 as a private, and would become a corporal and then a sergeant in Captain Richard Yancey's Co., Col. Glen's Virginia Regiment. He was appointed a Lieutenant in Captain Armistead White's Co., Col. Elias Edmund's Virginia Regiment. He was present at Yorktown.

He was according to the pension, born in Culpeper County, Virginia. He was living in Franklin County, Ky. in 1818. He died on 22 September 1837. Reference was made in the pension to eight children, but the only child named is Polly Clements, who survived her father. The name of his wife, her death, or his marriage to her is not stated in the pension.

His pension contains a form that mentions the Act of 6 April 1838. Whenever a pension contains this form it leads to additional information beyond the pension application file.

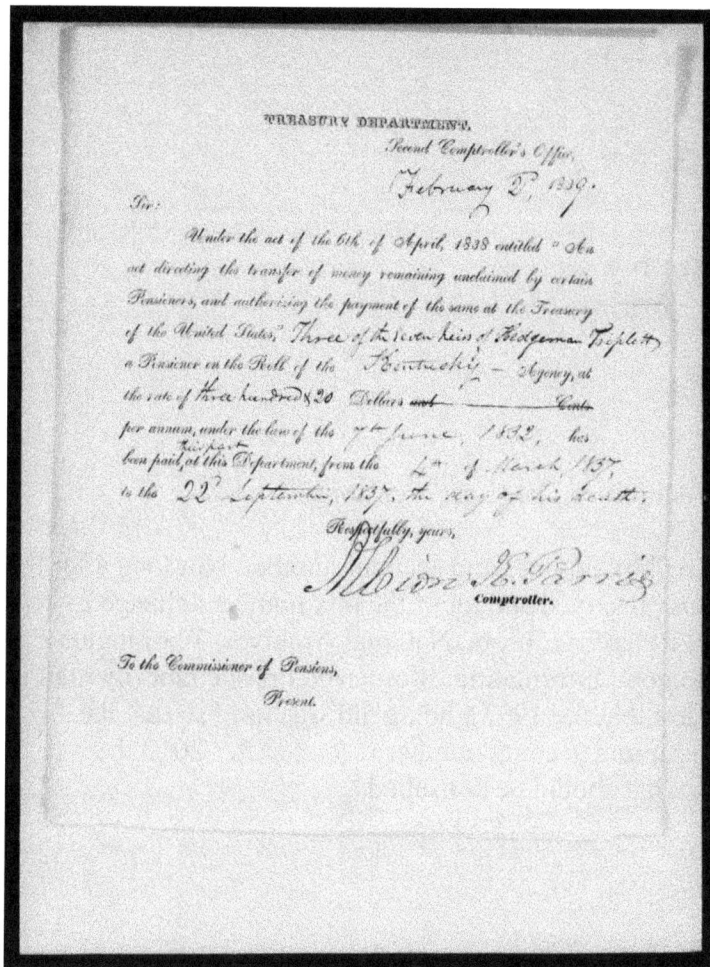

Sometimes a pension will contain a form that looks like the one above. This Treasury Department form leads to records among the settled accounts of 6 April 1838. Finding this form (and there may be more than one) informs the researcher that they must consult another source. ***The "Lost" Pensions: Settled Accounts of the Act of 6 April 1838*** is a finding aid to payment records found in the series of records entitled "Settled Accounts for Payment of the Accrued Pensions (Final Payments)" found in Entry 724 of the Records of the Third Auditor, Records of the Accounting Officers of the Department of the Treasury, Record Group 217, at the National Archives in Washington, D.C. They represent accounts from the Revolutionary War, War of 1812, a various Indian Wars before 1860, and the Mexican War. Many of the individuals identified in this list are not found in the pension indexes familiar to genealogists that cover the periods of those wars.

Triplett, Hedgeman, c/o, Ky.,
26, #5100
Triplett, Hedgeman, c/o, Ky.,
26, #7187
Triplett, Hedgeman, c/o, Ky.,
26, #8207
Triplett, Hedgemon, c/o, —, 60,
#8207, card

These are the entries from the first edition of The 'Lost' Pensions.

In this 1997 edition the material is by box number and account number. Not long after the book was published the material was preserved and all of the box numbers changed. There is a cross-walk in the Central Reference Room, National Archives, Washington, D.C. to convert the information into good information. If ordering the accounts by mail it is important to include in your request that the 1997 finding aid was used so that the information can be converted to a year and account number format. After 2013 the revised edition of the finding aid is what should be consulted.

TRIPLETT, Hedgeman, c/o,
Ky., 1839, #5100
TRIPLETT, Hedgeman, c/o,
Ky., 1839, #7187
TRIPLETT, Hedgeman, c/o,
Ky., 1840, #8207
TRIPLETT, Peter, c/o,
Richmond, Va., 1857,
#6070
TRIPLETT, Susannah,
Richmond, Va., #F6
[NF:VA]

These are the entries from the 2013 edition.

Because you find reference to the settled accounts of 1838 does not mean that you should skip the pension ledgers or the payment vouchers, including the last and final payments.

Consulting the Index to Final Payments on Fold3 reveals more than one entry which is unusually. Normally there is either a last or a final payment entry, not both.

NAME TRIPLETT, HEDGEMAN

AGENCY OF PAYMENT        KENTUCKY

DATE OF ACT        1832

DATE OF PAYMENT    2nd QUARTER 1837

DATE OF DEATH

LAST~~xxxxxxx~~ ~~FINAL~~ **PAYMENT VOUCHER RECEIVED FROM THE GENERAL ACCOUNTING OFFICE**

GENERAL SERVICES ADMINISTRATION        GSA DC 70-7035        FORM GSA DEC 69 **7068**

This is the last payment. Hedgeman has not yet died. The asterisk indicates that this payment can be found among the Last and Final Payment series.

NAME  TRIPLETT, ---Hedgeman

AGENCY OF PAYMENT  Ky.

DATE OF ACT  1832

DATE OF PAYMENT  1st qtr. 1839

DATE OF DEATH  Sept. 22, 1837

## FINAL PAYMENT VOUCHER RECEIVED FROM
## THE GENERAL ACCOUNTING OFFICE

GENERAL SERVICES ADMINISTRATION          GSA DC 70-7035          GSA FORM DEC 69 **7068**

This is the final payment. The payment is being made after Hedgeman has died. Note that there is no asterisk so this record will not be found in the series of Last and Final Payments. Although there is nothing on this card to tell us to go to the Settled Accounts of 6 April 1838 the form letter in the pension file does. Sometimes these slips will mention some combination of the terms in the phrase "Act of 6 April 1838".

Since with the exception of Georgia and Delaware whose last and final payments are on Fold3 a trip to the National Archives or hiring someone in D.C. to find the payment will be necessary. In the interim, you should also examine the pension ledger.

In looking at the pension ledger we find from Appendix B the following for Kentucky.

Kentucky

| Kentucky | ¤ | 1818 | 1818-32 | A | 424-467 | ¤ |
|---|---|---|---|---|---|---|
| ¤ | ¤ | 1818 | 1820-44 | C | 307-328 | ¤ |
| ¤ | ¤ | 1832 | 1833-48 | D | 326-358 | ¤ |
| ¤ | ¤ | 1818 | 1833-48 | E | 134-151 | ¤ |
| ¤ | ¤ | 1832 | 1831-48 | H | 223-254 | ¤ |
| ¤ | ¤ | 1832 | 1849-68 | I | 357-378 | ¤ |
| ¤ | ¤ | 1828 | 1831-48 | J | 321-324 | ¤ |
| ¤ | ¤ | Invalid | 1843-57 | K | 291-306 | ¤ |
| ¤ | ¤ | Invalid | 1855-66 | L-2 | 92-110 | ¤ |
| ¤ | ¤ | 1818 | 1848-61 | M | 103-104 | ¤ |
| ¤ | ¤ | 1828 | 1848-61 | M | 495-496 | ¤ |

Or we could use Ancestry

## Refine your search of the U.S. Pensioners, 1818-1872

☑ Exact matches only                                                     Search tips

| First Name | Last Name | Spelling |
|---|---|---|
| Hedgeman | Triplett | Exact ↕ |

**Widow**

| First Name | Last Name |
|---|---|
|  |  |

**Pension Office**

| State | City |
|---|---|
| Any ↕ | Any ↕ |

**Other**

| Year range | Keyword(s) |
|---|---|
| Any ↕ |  |

▲ **Hide Advanced Search Options**                                    Search

---

Unfortunately this is the return for this search:

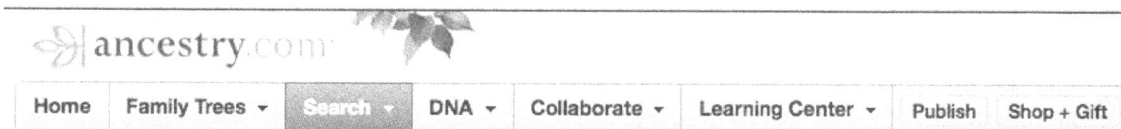

ancestry.com

| Home | Family Trees ▾ | Search ▾ | DNA ▾ | Collaborate ▾ | Learning Center ▾ | Publish | Shop + Gift |
|---|---|---|---|---|---|---|---|

### Your Search for **Hedgeman Triplett** returned no matches
### You searched for Hedgeman Triplett

Why?
Exact search only shows results that match **all** of your search criteria.
See Search Tips
What should you do?
Try removing search terms. This will increase your chances of getting a match on Exact Searches.
Try un-checking the 'Exact matches only' box to show close matches even when no exact matches are found.

☑ Exact matches only                                          Search tips

| First Name | Last Name | Spelling |
|---|---|---|
| Hedgeman | Triplett | Exact ↕ |

## Ranked Search Results - U.S. Pensioners, 1818-1872

You searched for **Hedgeman Triplett** Refine your search

Provided in
Association with

THE
NATIONAL
ARCHIVES
ARCHIVES.GOV

📑 All Military Results     Show  All matches     ⬍     Viewing **1-48**

| View Record | Name | Widow's Name | Pension Office City | Pension Office State | Year Range | View Image |
|---|---|---|---|---|---|---|
| View Record | **Peter Triplett** | | | Virginia | 1818-1832 | 🖼 |
| View Record | **Peter Triplett** | | | Virginia | 1818-1832 | 🖼 |
| View Record | **Daniel Triplett** | | | Virginia | 1831-1848 | 🖼 |
| View Record | **??Man Triplett** | | | Kentucky | 1831-1848 | 🖼 |
| View Record | **Peter Triplett** | | | Virginia | 1833-1849 | 🖼 |

# U.S. Pensioners, 1818-1872 record for ??Man Triplett

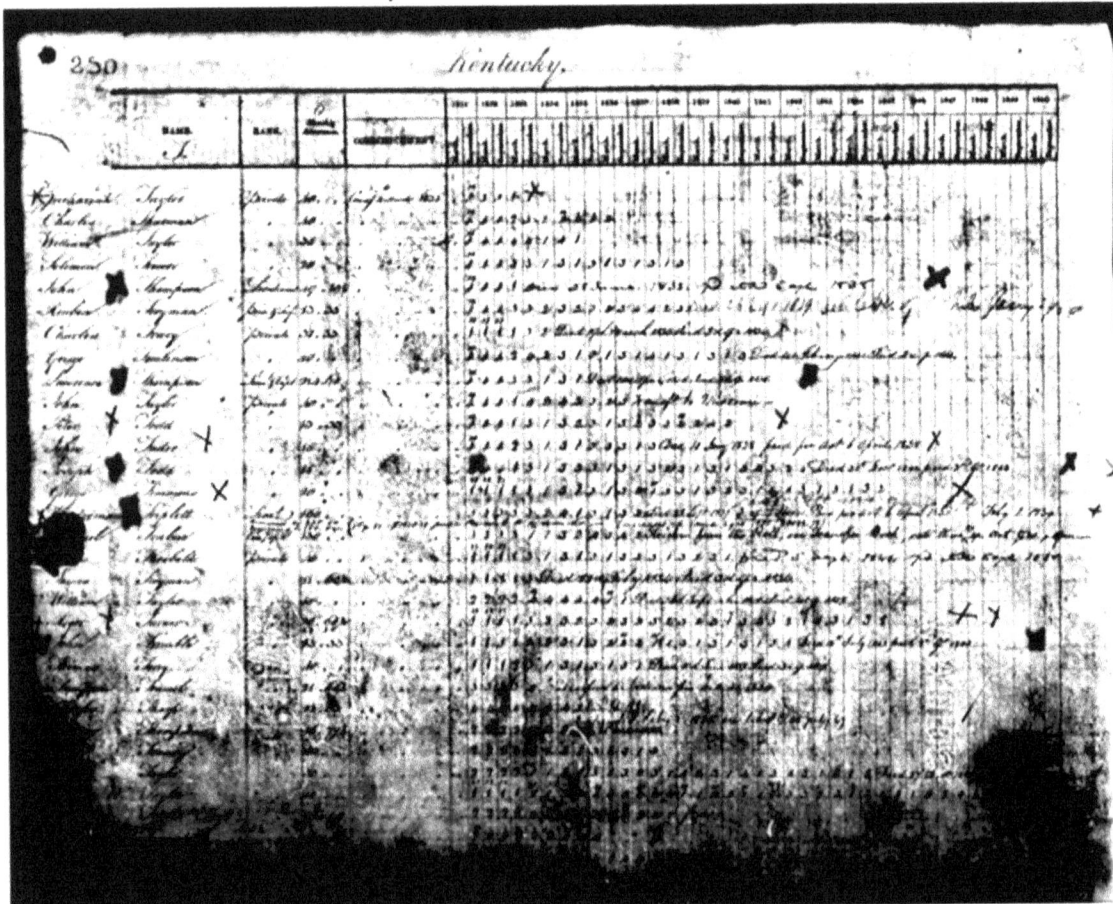

Searching by the surname alone in the U.S. Pensioners records get you to the correct place. You will find ???man Triplett under the large ink blot in the name column.

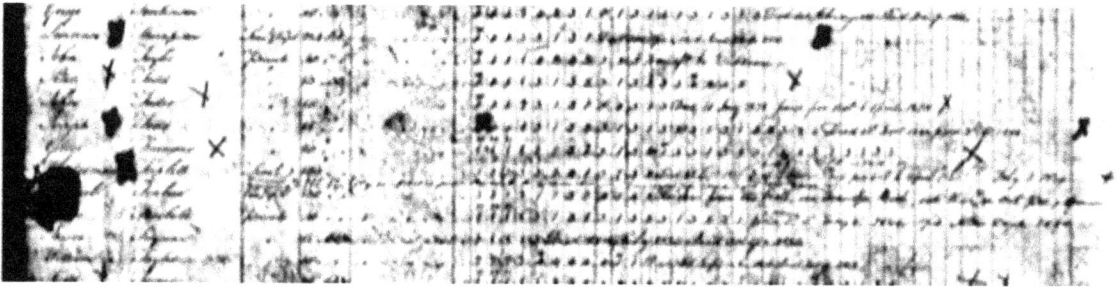

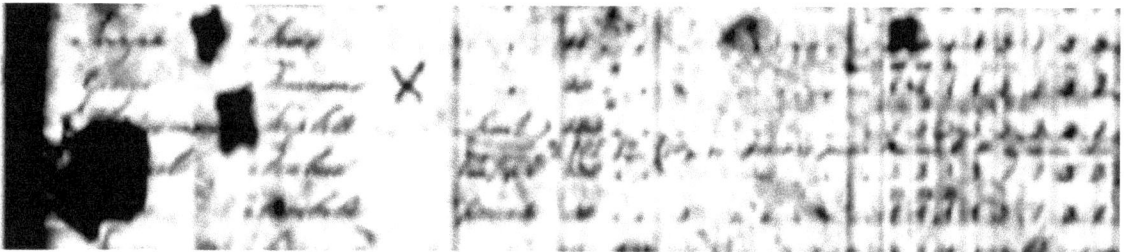

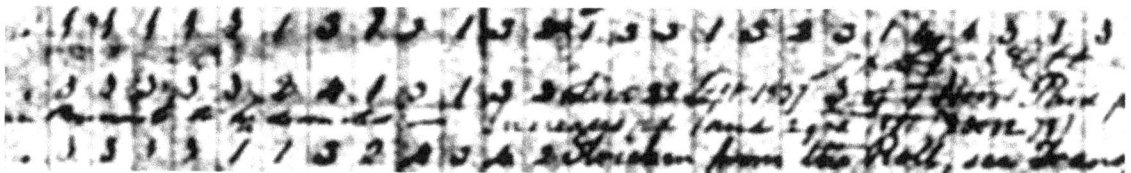

The Final Payment

In the case of Hedgeman Triplett there are several final payments because of the number of children who do not live close to each other. The documents show that:

He died 22 September 1837 at his residence in Franklin Co., Ky. He left no widow. But had the following heirs:
William Triplett, Franklin Co., Ky.
Hedgemen Triplett, Franklin Co., Ky.
Nancy Poe, wife of Edmund Poe, do
Elizabeth Grant, wife of Thomas Grant, do
George W. Triplett, Daviess Co., Ky.
Polly Clements, wife of Allen Clements

Children of Lucy Palmer, dec'd.
  Elizabeth Palmer, Indiana
  Nancy Palmer, Indiana
  Phebe Palmer, Indiana
  Thomas Palmer, Indiana
  Polly Palmer, Indiana
  William Palmer, Shelby Co., Ky.
  John Palmer, Shelby Co., Ky.
  Richard Palmer, Shelby Co., Ky.
  Hedgeman Palmer, Louisana
  Mildred Wright, wife of Abner Wright, Illinois

No. 5100

Triplett, Hedgeman

( Child of )

Kentucky

Act 6 April 1838

July 4 - 1839

State of Kentucky Franklin County Sct.
At a County Court held for the County
of Franklin at the Court House
in the Town of Frankfort on the
16th day of October 1837 —

On the motion of the heirs of Benjamin
Bartlett deceased, administration of the goods
and chattels rights and Credits of Benjamin
Bartlett deceased (the heirs refusing to act)
is granted to Diana Marqate Esqr Whereupon
he took the Oath prescribed by law and entered
into bond in the penalty of thirty thousand
dollars, with William Bartlett, George M Bartlett,
Edmond Co Edward Herndon and Lewis
Sanders, his securities Conditioned according
to law —

       A Copy, attest —

State of Kentucky Franklin County Sct.
At a County Court held for the County
of Franklin On the 20th day of
November 1837, at the Court house in
the Town of Frankfort —

It was proven to the satisfaction of the Court
that Benjamin Bartlett sene deceased, that
Commoner of the United States departed this
life on the 22d day of September 1837, at
his residence in this County of Franklin that
he left no widow but left the following named
persons as his children and _____ of them

Triplett, Hodgeman Triplett, Nancy Pea wife of
Edmund Pea, Elizabeth Grant wife of Thomas Grant
who reside in Franklin County Kentucky. George W.
Triplett who resided in Daviess County Kentucky
John Triplett who resided in the State of Missouri
Polly Clements wife of Allen Clements deceased
wife of late ~~Thomas~~ Elizabeth Palmer, Nancy
wife of late Nancy Palmer, Phebe
wife of late Phebe Palmer, Thomas
Palmer, Polly Palmer, the five last named being
Children of Lucy Palmer who was one of the
Children of said Hodgeman Triplett and is dead
who resided in the State of Indiana, William
Palmer, John Palmer and Richard Palmer
are children of the said Lucy Palmer decd
who reside in Shelby County Kentucky, Hodgeman
Palmer who is a child of said Lucy Palmer decd
who resided in the State of Tennessee, Milly
Wright wife of Thomas Wright who reside in the
State of Illinois which is ordered to be
recorded.

A Copy Attest.

J. H. Hanna Clk

# Appendix A

## Pension Ledger Microfilm Roll Listing

| Roll | Volume | | Description | Years |
|------|--------|---|-------------|-------|
| 1 | A | | Revolutionary War Pensioners Under the Act of 1818 | 1818-32 |
| 2 | B | | Revolutionary War Pensioners Under the Act of 1818 | 1818-32 |
| 3 | C | | Revolutionary War Pensioners and Invalid Pensioners of the War of 1812 Under the Act of 1818 | 1820-42 |
| 4 | D | | Revolutionary War Pensioners Under the Act of 1818 and 1832 | 1833-48 |
| 5 | E | | Revolutionary War Pensioners Under the Act of 1818 and 1832 | 1833-49 |
| 6 | F | | Revolutionary War Pensioners Under the Act of 1832 | 1831-48 |
| 7 | G | | Revolutionary War Pensioners Under the Act of 1832 | 1831-48 |
| 8 | H | | Revolutionary War Pensioners Under the Act of 1832 | 1831-48 |
| 9 | I | | Revolutionary War Pensioners Under the Act of 1832 | 1849-64 |
| 10 | J | | Revolutionary War Pensioners Under the Act of 1818, 1828, and 1832 | 1831-50 |
| 11 | K | | Invalid Pensions | 1843-56 |
| 12 | L-1 | | Invalid Pensions | 1855-67 |
| 13 | L-2 | | Invalid Pensions | 1855-66 |
| 14 | M | | Revolutionary War Pensioners Under the | 1848-68 |

| | | | | |
|---|---|---|---|---|
| | | | Act of 1818, 1828, and 1853 (2d Sec.) | |
| | | | | |
| 15 | N | | Widow Pensions Under the Act of July 4, 1836 | 1831-43 |
| | | | | |
| 16 | O | | Widow Pensions Under the Act of July 4, 1836 | 1843-62 |
| | | | | |
| 17 | P | | Widow Pensions Under the Act of July 7, 1838, March 3, 1843, and February 2, 1848 | 1836-48 |
| | | | | |
| 18 | Q | | Widow Pensions Under the Act of July 7, 1838, March 3, 1843, and June 17, 1844 | 1836-50 |
| | | | | |
| 19 | R | | Widow Pensions Under the Acts of February 2 and July 29, 1848 | 1848-62 |
| | | | | |
| 20 | S | | Widow Pensions Under the Acts of February 2, 1848 | 1848-62 |
| | | | | |
| 21 | T | | Widow Pensions Under the Acts of July 4, 1836, and July 21, 1848, February 2 and July 29, 1848, and February 3, 1853 (2nd Sec.) | 1862-72 |
| | | | | |
| 22 | U | | Widow Pensions Under the Act of February 3, 1853 (1st Sec.) | 1853-72 |
| | | | | |
| 23 | V | | Widow Pensions Under the Act of February 3, 1853 (2nd Sec.) and June 3, 1858 | 1858-72 |

# Appendix B

## Pension Office Listing

### Alabama

| Agency | Location | Act or Acts | Period of Payment | Volume | Pages |
|---|---|---|---|---|---|
| Alabama | | 1818 | 1818-32 | B | 432-439 |
| | Decatur | 1818 | 1820-44 | C | 591-592 |
| | | 1818 | 1831-48 | J | 193-197 |
| | | 1828 | 1831-48 | J | 317 only |
| | | 1832 | 1831-48 | G | 434-439 |
| | Huntsville | 1832 | 1849-68 | I | 299-302 |
| | | 1832 | 1831-48 | G | 440 only |
| | | Invalid | 1843-57 | K | 237-240 |
| | | Invalid | 1855-66 | L-1 | 268-271 |
| | | 1818 | 1848-61 | M | 81-84 |
| | | 1828 | 1848-61 | M [omitted] | 473-474 |
| | | 1853 | 1853-61 | M | 343-344 |
| | | 1836 | 1831-43 | N | 220 only |
| | | 1836 | 1844-63 | O | 197-200 |
| | | 1838, 1843, 1844 | 1836-48 | Q | 179-182a |
| | | 1848 | 1848-61 | R | 1-4 |
| | | 1836,1848 | 1862-70 | T | 31 only |
| | | 1853 (1st Sec.) | 1853-57 | U | 282-285 |
| | | 1858 | 1858-70 | V | 155-157 |
| | Mobile | 1818 | 1820-44 | C | 463-474 |
| | | 1818 | 1833-48 | E | 121-123 |
| | | 1832 | 1831-48 | H | 418-437 |
| | | 1832 | 1849-68 | I | 307-312 |
| | | 1828 | 1831-48 | J | 316 only |
| | | Invalid | 1843-57 | K | 245-247 |
| | | Invalid | 1855-66 | L-1 | 272-275 |
| | | 1818 | 1848-61 | M | 85-88 |
| | | 1828 | 1848-61 | M | 47-478 |
| | | 1853 | 1853-61 | M | 339-340 |
| | | 1836 | 1831-43 | N | 220-221 |
| | | 1836 | 1844-53 | O | 197-200 |
| | | 1838,1843,1844 | 1836-48 | Q | 163-171 |
| | | 1848 | 1848-61 | R | 5-6 |
| | | 1836,1848 | 1862-70 | T | 30 only |

| | | | | | |
|---|---|---|---|---|---|
| | | 1853 (1st Sec.) | 1853-57 | U | 274-277 |
| | | 1858 | 1858-70 | V | 151-154 |
| | Tuscaloosa | 1818 | 1820-44 | C | 620-621 |
| | | 1832 | 183348 | F | 163-171 |
| | | 1832 | 1849-68 | I | 303-306 |
| | | 1818 | 1831-48 | J | 257-258 |
| | | 1828 | 1831-48 | J | 316 only |
| | | Invalid | 1843-57 | K | 241-244 |
| | | Invalid | 1855-66 | L-1 | 276-278 |
| | | 1828 | 1848-61 | M | 475-476 |
| | | 1853 | 1853-61 | M | 341-342 |
| | | 1836 | 1831-43 | N | 222 only |
| | | 1836 | 1844-53 | O | 199 only |
| | | 1838,1843-1844 | 1836-48 | Q | 173-178 |
| | | 1848 | 184-61 | R | 7-10 |
| | | 1836,1848 | 1862-70 | T | 32 only |
| | | 1853 (1st Sec.) | 1853-57 | U | 278-281 |
| | | 1858 | 1858-70 | V | 185-160 |

Arkansas

| | | | | | |
|---|---|---|---|---|---|
| Arkansas | | 1818 | 1820-44 | C | 579-584 |
| | | 1832 | 1831-48 | G | 420-424 |
| | | 1818,1828,1832 | 1831-48 | J | 208-211, 333 only |
| | | 1832 | 1849-68 | I | 431-432 |
| | | Invalid | 1843-57 | K | 258-261 |
| | | 1828 | 1848-61 | M | 483-484 |
| | | 1853 | 1853-61 | M | 353-354 |
| | | 1836 | 1844-60 | O | 209-212 |
| | | 1838,1843,1844 | 1836-48 | Q | 335-340 |
| | | 1848 | 1848-61 | R | 11-16 |
| | | 1848 | 1862-70 | T | 185-186 |
| | | 1836,1848 | 1862-70 | T | 35 only |
| | | 1853 (1st Sec.) | 1853-57 | U | 304-09 |
| | | 1858 | 1858-70 | V | 169-170 |
| | Fort Gibson | Invalid | 1843-57 | K | 362-363 |
| | | Invalid | 1855-66 | L-2 | 27-28 |
| | | 1858 | 1859-70 | V | 169-174 |
| | Little Rock | 1818 | 1831-48 | J | 210-211 |
| | | Invalid | 1855-66 | L-2 | 21-26 |
| | | 1853 (2nd Sec.) | 1858-70 | V | 498-499 |

## California

| California | | Invalid | 1843-57 | K | 452-454 |
|---|---|---|---|---|---|
| | | Invalid | 1855-66 | L-2 | 250-255 |
| | | 1836, 1848 | 1862-70 | T | 57 only |
| | | 1848 | 1862-70 | T | 233 only |
| | | 1853 (1st Sec.) | 1853-57 | U | 295-296 |
| | San Francisco | 1858 | 1858-70 | V | 165 only |

## Connecticut

| Connecticut | | 1818 | 1818-32 | B | 180-238 |
|---|---|---|---|---|---|
| | | 1818 | 1818-32 | B | 489 only |
| | | 1818 | 1820-44 | C | 48-65 |
| | | 1818 | 183-48 | D | 139-168 |
| | | 1832 | 1833-48 | E | 422-446 |
| | | 1832 | 1831-48 | H | 77-140 |
| | | 1832 | 1849-68 | I | 97-118 |
| | | 1818,1828,1832 | 1831-48 | J | 281-283 |
| | | Invalid | 1843-57 | K | 73-81 |
| | | Invalid | 1855-66 | L-1 | 64-70 |
| | | 1818 | 1848-61 | M | 37-40 |
| | | 1828 | 1848-61 | M | 439-440 |
| | | 1853 | 1853-61 | M | 199-214 |
| | | 1836 | 1831-43 | N | 76-87, 163-167,169-177 |
| | | 1836 | 1844-53 | O | 65-80 |
| | | 1838,1843,1848 | 1836-48 | P | 215-258 |
| | | 1848 | 1848-61 | R | 17-72 |
| | | 1836,1848 | 1862-70 | T | 10 only |
| | | 1848 | 1862-70 | T | 117-122 |
| | | 1853 (1st Sec.) | 1853-57 | U | 81-96 |
| | Hartford | 1858 | 1858-70 | V | 29-32 |
| | | 1853 (2nd Sec.) | 1862-70 | T | 272-275 |

## Delaware

| Delaware | | 1818 | 1818-32 | A | 291-312 |
|---|---|---|---|---|---|
| | | 1818 | 1820-44 | C | 189-198 |
| | | 1818 | 1833-48 | E | 63-64 |
| | | 1832 | 1831-48 | G | 418-419 |
| | | 1832 | 1849-68 | I | 231-234 |

| | | | | | |
|---|---|---|---|---|---|
| | | 1828 | 1831-48 | J | 305 only |
| | | Invalid | 1843-57 | K | 181-184 |
| | | 1828 | 1848-61 | M | 453-456 |
| | | 1853 | 1853-61 | M | 291-292 |
| | | 1836 | 1831-43 | N | 213 only |
| | | 1836 | 1844-60 | O | 147 only |
| | | 1838,1843,1844 | 1836-48 | Q | 48-50 |
| | | 1848 | 1848-61 | R | 75-78 |
| | Dover (changed to Wilmington) | 1858 | 1858-70 | V | 65-68 |
| | | 1853 (2nd Sec.) | 1858-70 | V | 414-416 |

District of Columbia

| | | | | | |
|---|---|---|---|---|---|
| District of Columbia | | 1818 | 1818-32 | B | 448-461 |
| | | 1818 | 1820-44 | C | 382-395 |
| | | 1818 | 1833-48 | E | 70-71 |
| | | 1832 | 1831-48 | H | 410-417 |
| | | 1832 | 1849-68 | I | 239-242 |
| | | 1832 | 1831-48 | J | 333 only |
| | | Invalid | 1843-57 | K | 180 only, 184-192, 419-421 |
| | | Invalid | 1855-66 | L-1 | 209-225 |
| | | 1818 | 1848-61 | M | 65-66 |
| | | 1828 | 1848-61 | M | 457-458 |
| | | 1853 (2nd Sec.) | 1853-61 | M | 311-316 |
| | | 1836 | 1831-43 | N | 122-123 |
| | | 1836 | 1844-60 | O | 163-168 |
| | | 1838,1843,1844 | 1836-48 | Q | 355-360 |
| | | 1848 | 1848-61 | R | 79-84 |
| | | 1836,1848 | 1862-70 | T | 20-21, 25 only |
| | | 1848 | 1862-70 | T | 152-154 |
| | | 1853 (1st Sec.) | 1853-57 | U | 201-213 |
| | | 1858 | 1858-70 | V | 83-90, 101-102, 147-148 |
| | | 1853 (2nd Sec.) | 1858-70 | V | 361 only, 371 only, 503-508 |

# Florida

| Florida | Jacksonville | 1818 | 1831-48 | J | 203 only |
|---|---|---|---|---|---|
| | | 1832 | 1849-68 | I | 295-298 |
| | | Invalid | 1843-57 | K | 227-231 |
| | | Invalid | 1855-66 | L-2 | 2-5 |
| | | 1828 | 1848-61 | M | 469-470 |
| | | 1853 (2$^{nd}$ Sec.) | 1853-61 | M | 335-336 |
| | | 1836 | 1831-43 | N | 227 only |
| | | 1836 | 1844-60 | O | 192-193 |
| | | 1838,1843,1844 | 1836-48 | Q | 347-349 |
| | | 1848 | 1848-61 | R | 86-88 |
| | | 1836,1848 | 1862-70 | T | 28 only |
| | | 1853 (1$^{st}$ Sec.) | 1853-57 | U | 266-269 |
| | | 1858 | 1858-70 | V | 145-146 |
| | St. Augustine | 1818 | 1820-44 | C | 593-594 |
| | | 1818 | 1831-48 | J | 201-203 |
| | | 1832 | 1832-48 | G | 444-446 |
| | | Invalid | 1843-57 | K | 227-231 |
| | | 1836 | 1831-43 | N | 227-228 |
| | | 1836 | 1844-60 | O | 192-193 |
| | Tallahassee | 1818 | 1820-44 | C | 617-619 |
| | | 1832 | 1833-48 | F | 128-134 |
| | | 1832 | 149-68 | I | 291-294 |
| | | Invalid | 1843-57 | K | 233-236 |
| | | 1828 | 1848-61 | M | 471-72 |
| | | 1853 (2$^{nd}$ Sec.) | 1853-61 | M | 337-338 |
| | | 1836 | 1831-43 | N | 226 only |
| | | 1836 | 1844-53 | O | 194-196, 431-433 |
| | | 1838,1843,1844 | 1836-48 | Q | 350-51 |
| | | 1848 | 1848-61 | R | 89-92 |
| | | 1836,1848 | 1862-70 | T | 29 only |
| | | 1853 (1$^{st}$ Sec.) | 1853-57 | U | 270-73 |
| | | 1858 | 1858-70 | V | 141-144 |

# Georgia

| Georgia | | 1818 | 1818-72 | B | 361-376 |
|---|---|---|---|---|---|
| | | 1818 | 1820-44 | C | 287-306 |
| | | 1818 | 1833-48 | E | 117-120 |
| | | 1832 | 1833-48 | E | 402-421 |
| | | 1832 | 1831-48 | H | 380-393 |
| | | 1832 | 1849-68 | I | 283-290 |

| | | 1832 | 1831-48 | J | 315 only |
|---|---|---|---|---|---|
| | | Invalid | 1843-57 | K | 220-226 |
| | | Invalid | 1855-66 | L-1 | 256-267 |
| | | 1818 | 1848-61 | M | 75-80 |
| | | 1828 | 1848-61 | M | 467-468 |
| | | 1853 | 1853-61 | M | 329-334 |
| | | 1836 | 1831-43 | N | 134-135 |
| | | 1836 | 1844-60 | O | 188-191, 274-277 |
| | | 1838,1843,1844 | 1836-48 | Q | 149-162 |
| | | 1848 | 1848-61 | R | 93-100 |
| | | 1848 | 1862-70 | T | 174-175 |
| | | 1836,1848 | 1862-70 | T | 27 only |
| | | 1853 (1st Sec.) | 1853-57 | U | 256-265 |
| | Savannah | 1858 | 1858-70 | V | 123-128 |

Illinois

| | | 1818 | 1818-32 | B | 424-431 |
|---|---|---|---|---|---|
| Illinois | | 1818 | 1820-44 | C | 451-462 |
| | | 1818 | 1833-48 | E | 177-179 |
| | | 1832 | 1831-48 | E | 447-454 |
| | | 1832 | 1831-48 | H | 403-409 |
| | | 1832 | 1849-68 | I | 379-384 |
| | | 1828 | 1831-48 | J | 331 only |
| | | Invalid | 1843-57 | K | 325-334, 371-374, 412-417 |
| | | 1818 | 1848-61 | M | 107-108 |
| | | 1828 | 1848-61 | M | 501-503 |
| | | 1853 | 1853-61 | M | 414 only |
| | | 1836 | 1831-43 | N | 129 only |
| | | 1836 | 1844-53 | O | 253-256, 305-331 |
| | | 1838,1843,1844 | 1836-48 | Q | 319-326 |
| | | 1848 | 1848-61 | R | 117-123 |
| | Cairo (changed to Salem) | 1836,1848 | 1862-70 | T | 62 only |
| | | 1848 | 1862-70 | T | 238 only |
| | | 1853 (2nd Sec.) | 1853-57 | U | 475-480 |
| | Cairo (changed to Centralia) | 1858 | 1858-70 | V | 343-49 |

| | | | | | |
|---|---|---|---|---|---|
| | | 1853 (2nd Sec.) | 1858-70 | V | 401-10 |
| | Chicago | Invalid | 1855-66 | L-2 | 201-218 |
| | | 1853 | 1853-61 | M | 347-348 |
| | | 1836,1848 | 1862-70 | M | 457-458 |
| | | 1848 | 1862-70 | T | 65 only |
| | | 1853 (1st Sec.) | 1853-57 | U | 464-66 |
| | | 1858 | 1858-70 | V | 301-308 |
| | | 1853 (2nd Sec.) | 1858-70 | V | 362-63 |
| | Quincy | 1858 | 1858-70 | V | 491 only |
| | | 1853 (2nd Sec.) | 1858-70 | V | 492 only |
| | Springfield | Invalid | 1855-66 | L-1 | 209-225 |
| | | 1853 | 1853-61 | M | 383-384 |
| | | 1853 (2nd Sec.) | 1853-61 | M | 500 only |
| | | 1848 | 1862-70 | T | 213-215 |
| | | 1836,1848 | 1862-70 | T | 47-48 |
| | | 1853 (1st Sec.) | 1853-57 | U | 382-97 |
| | | 1858 | 1858-70 | V | 243-51 |
| | | 1853 (2nd Sec.) | 1858-70 | V | 368-69 |

Indiana

| | | | | | |
|---|---|---|---|---|---|
| Indiana | | 1818 | 1818-32 | B | 377-394 |
| | | 1818 | 1820-44 | C | 405-416 |
| | | 1818 | 1833-48 | E | 170-176 |
| | | 1832 | 1831-48 | G | 357-385 |
| | | 1832 | 1849-68 | I | 385-394 |
| | | 1828 | 1831-48 | J | 329-330 |
| | | Invalid | 1843-57 | K | 397-402 |
| | | 1818 | 1848-61 | M | 105-106 |
| | | 1828 | 1848-61 | M | 457-458 |
| | | 1836 | 1831-43 | N | 128 only |
| | | 1836 | 1844-53 | O | 257-260 |
| | | 1836 | 1844-60 | O | 285-302 |
| | Evansville | 1832 | 1849-68 | I | 439-440 |
| | | Invalid | 1843-57 | K | 467-470 |
| | | 1853 (2nd Sec.) | 1853-61 | M | 377-378 |
| | | 1836 | 1844-53 | O | 461-464 |
| | | 1848 | 1848-61 | S | 329-332 |
| | (changed to Fort Wayne) | 1853 (1st Sec.) | 1853-57 | U | 364-69 |
| | Fort Wayne | Invalid | 1855-66 | L-2 | 264-268 |
| | | 1853 (2nd Sec.) | 1853-61 | M | 415-416 |
| | | 1836 | 1844-53 | O | 303 only |
| | | 1836,1848 | 1862-70 | T | 50 only |
| | | 1848 | 1862-70 | T | 219 only |

| | | 1858 | 1858-70 | V | 287-290 |
|---|---|---|---|---|---|
| | | 1853 (2nd Sec.) | 1858-70 | V | 481-482 |
| | Indianapolis | Invalid | 1843-57 | K | 335-343 |
| | | Invalid | 1855-66 | L-2 | 147-159 |
| | Indianapolis and Madison | 1853 (2nd Sec.) | 1853-61 | M | 377-378, 380-383, 406 only |
| | | 1848 | 1848-61 | R | 101-110 |
| | | 1836, 1848 | 1862-70 | T | 49 only, 58 only |
| | | 1848 | 1862-70 | T | 152-154 |
| | | 1853 (1st Sec.) | 1853-71 | U | 374-81 |
| | | 1858 | 1858-70 | V | 233-238 |
| | | 1853 (2nd Sec.) | 1858-70 | V | 383-385 |
| | Indianapolis, New Albany, and Madison | Invalid | 1843-57 | K | 335 |
| | | Invalid | 1855-66 | L-2 | 160-169 |
| | | 1853 | 1853-61 | M | 406 only |
| | | 1838, 1843, 1844 | 1836-48 | Q | 299-314 |
| | | 1836, 1848 | 1862-70 | T | 61 only |
| | | 1848 | 1862-70 | T | 220 only |
| | | 1858 | 1858-70 | V | 242 only |
| | | 1853 (2nd Sec.) | 1858-70 | V | 19-23 |
| | (transferred to | Invalid | 1855-66 | L-2 | 170-175 |
| | Indianapolis in 1861) | 1853 (2nd Sec.) | 1853-61 | M | 379-380 |
| | | 1838, 1843, 1844 | 1836-48 | Q | 315-318 |
| | | 1848 | 1848-61 | R | 111-116 |
| | | 1853 (1st Sec.) | 1853-57 | U | 370-73 |
| | | 1858 | 1858-70 | V | 239-241 |

Iowa

| | | 1818 | 1820-44 | C | 622 only |
|---|---|---|---|---|---|
| Iowa | | 1832 | 1833-48 | F | 172-176 |
| | | 1832 | 1849-68 | I | 423-426 |
| | | Invalid | 1843-57 | K | 316-320 |
| | | Invalid | 1855-66 | L-2 | 244-249 |
| | | 1818 | 1848-61 | M | 111-112 |
| | | 1828 | 1848-61 | M | 505-506 |
| | | 1853 (2nd Sec.) | 1853-61 | M | 409-410 |
| | | 1836 | 1844-53 | O | 245-246 |
| | | 1838, 1843, 1844 | 1836-48 | Q | 368-371 |

|  |  | 1848 | 1848-61 | R | 124-128 |
|---|---|---|---|---|---|
|  |  | 1836,1848 | 1862-70 | T | 45 only |
|  |  | 1848 | 1862-70 | T | 208-209 |
|  |  | 1853 (1st Sec.) | 1853-57 | U | 450-457 |
|  | Des Moines | 1836,1848 | 1862-70 | T | 45 only |
|  |  | 1858 | 1858-70 | V | 269-71 |
|  |  | 1853 (2nd Sec.) | 1858-70 | V | 382 only |
|  | Dubuque (changed to Marion) | 1858 | 1858-70 | V | 393-395 |
|  |  | 1853 (2nd Sec.) | 1858-70 | V | 393-395 |
|  | Fairfield | 1853 (2nd Sec.) | 1863-65 | M | 418-420 |
|  |  | 1853 (2nd Sec.) | 1858-70 | V | 411-13 |
|  |  | 1858 | 1858-70 | V | 340-342 |
|  | Mason City | 1853 (1st Sec.) | 1853-57 | U | 487 only |

## Kansas

| Kansas |  | Invalid | 1855-66 | L-2 | 269-274 |
|---|---|---|---|---|---|
|  |  | 1836,1848 | 1862-70 | T | 59 only |
|  |  | 1848 | 1862-70 | T | 152-154 |
|  | Topeka | 1858 | 1858-70 | V | 272 only |

## Kentucky

| Kentucky |  | 1818 | 1818-32 | A | 424-467 |
|---|---|---|---|---|---|
|  |  | 1818 | 1820-44 | C | 307-328 |
|  |  | 1832 | 1833-48 | D | 326-358 |
|  |  | 1818 | 1833-48 | E | 134-151 |
|  |  | 1832 | 1831-48 | H | 223-254 |
|  |  | 1832 | 1849-68 | I | 357-378 |
|  |  | 1828 | 1831-48 | J | 321-324 |
|  |  | Invalid | 1843-57 | K | 291-306 |
|  |  | Invalid | 1855-66 | L-2 | 92-110 |
|  |  | 1818 | 1848-61 | M | 103-104 |
|  |  | 1828 | 1848-61 | M | 495-496 |
|  |  | 1853 (2nd Sec.) | 1853-61 | M | 350-352, 371-376 |
|  |  | 1836 | 1836-43 | N | 126-127, 212 only, 219 only |
|  |  | 1836 | 1844-60 | O | 232-240 |
|  |  | 1838,1843,1844 | 1836-48 | Q | 229-272 |

| | | 1848 | 1848-61 | R | 129-152 |
|---|---|---|---|---|---|
| | | 1836,1848 | 1862-70 | T | 42-43 |
| | | 1853 (1st Sec.) | 1853-57 | U | 348-63 |
| | | 1858 | 1858-70 | V | 223-232 |
| | Lexington | 1836 | 1844-53 | O | 406-408 |
| | | 1848 | 1862-70 | T | 135-136 |
| | | 1836,1848 | 1862-70 | T | 41 only |
| | | 1853 (1st Sec.) | 1853-57 | U | 481-84 |
| | | 1858 | 1858-70 | V | 443-452 |
| | Louisville | 1836,1848 | 1862-70 | T | 42-43 |
| | | 1848 | 1862-70 | T | 200-204 |
| | | 1858 | 1858-70 | V | 223-232 |
| | | 1853 (2nd Sec.) | 1858-70 | V | 364-67 |

## Louisiana

| | | 1818 | 1818-32 | B | 440-447 |
|---|---|---|---|---|---|
| Louisiana | | 1818 | 1820-44 | C | 396-404 |
| | | 1818 | 1833-48 | E | 184-185 |
| | | 1832 | 1831-48 | G | 404-411 |
| | | 1832 | 1849-68 | I | 317-320 |
| | | 1832 | 1831-48 | J | 334 only |
| | | Invalid | 1843-57 | K | 232 only, 248-254, 257-258 |
| | | Invalid | 1855-66 | L-2 | 9-20 |
| | | 1828 | 1848-61 | M | 479-480 |
| | | 1853 (2nd Sec.) | 1853-61 | M | 345-346 |
| | | 1836 | 1844-53 | O | 201-204 |
| | | 1838,1843,1844 | 1836-48 | Q | 352-354 |
| | | 1848 | 1848-61 | R | 153-156 |
| | | 1836,1848 | 1862-70 | T | 33 only |
| | | 1848 | 1862-70 | T | 181-182 |
| | | 1853 (1st Sec.) | 1853-57 | U | 266-292 |
| | New Orleans | 1858 | 1858-70 | V | 137-140 |
| | | 1853 (2nd Sec.) | 1858-70 | V | 497 only |

## Maine

| | | 1818 | 1818-32 | B | 98-179 |
|---|---|---|---|---|---|
| Maine | | 1818 | 1820-44 | C | 35-47 |
| | | 1818 | 1833-48 | E | 1-46 |
| | | 1832 | 1831-48 | H | 1-76 |
| | | 1828 | 1831-48 | J | 270-273 |

| | | Invalid | 1843-57 | K | 1-14 |
|---|---|---|---|---|---|
| | | 1818 | 1848-61 | M | 1-8 |
| | | 1828 | 1848-61 | M | 425-426 |
| | | 1836 | 1831-43 | N | 50-56, 214-217 |
| | | 1836 | 1844-53 | O | 1-10 |
| | | 1838,1843,1844 | 1836-48 | P | 2-42 |
| | | 1848 | 1848-61 | R | 259-312 |
| | | 1836,1848 | 1862-70 | T | 1-2 |
| | Augusta | 1832 | 1849-68 | I | 1-17 |
| | | Invalid | 1855-66 | L-1 | 1-18 |
| | | 1853 (2$^{nd}$ Sec.) | 1853-61 | M | 133-147 |
| | | 1853 (1$^{st}$ Sec.) | 1853-57 | U | 1-21 |
| | | 1848 | 1862-70 | T | 83-87 |
| | | 1853 (2$^{nd}$ Sec.) | 1862-70 | T | 254-257 |
| | | 1858 | 1858-70 | V | 1-4, 293-294 |
| | Bangor | 1848 | 1862-70 | T | 88 only |
| | | 1853 (1$^{st}$ Sec.) | 1853-57 | U | 488 only |
| | | 1858 | 1858-70 | V | 283-86 |
| | | 1853 (2$^{nd}$ Sec.) | 1858-70 | V | 485-90 |
| | Portland | 1832 | 1849-68 | I | 18 only |
| | | 1853 (2$^{nd}$ Sec.) | 1853-61 | M | 126-132 |
| | | 1848 | 1862-70 | T | 242-245 |
| | | 1853 (1$^{st}$ Sec.) | 1853-57 | U | 470-474 |
| | | 1853 (2$^{nd}$ Sec.) | 1862-70 | T | 250-253 |
| | | 1858 | 1858-70 | V | 311-318 |

Maryland

| Maryland | | 1818 | 1818-32 | A | 313-365 |
|---|---|---|---|---|---|
| | | 1818 | 1820-44 | C | 199-224 |
| | | 1818 | 1833-48 | E | 65-69 |
| | | 1832 | 1831-48 | H | 320-339 |
| | | 1832 | 1849-68 | I | 235-238 |
| | | 1832 | 1831-48 | J | 306-307 |
| | | Invalid | 1843-57 | K | 171-180 |
| | | Invalid | 1855-66 | L-1 | 199-208 |
| | | 1818 | 1848-61 | M | 63-64 |
| | | 1828 | 1848-61 | M | 455-456 |
| | | 1853 (2$^{nd}$ Sec.) | 1853-61 | M | 293-296 |
| | | 1836 | 1831-43 | N | 118-119 |
| | | 1836 | 1844-53 | O | 149-152 |
| | | 1838,1843,1844 | 1836-48 | Q | 51-64 |
| | | 1848 | 1848-61 | R | 313-322 |

| | | | | | |
|---|---|---|---|---|---|
| | | 1836,1848 | 1862-70 | T | 19 only |
| | | 1848 | 1862-70 | T | 149-151 |
| | | 1853 (1st Sec.) | 1853-57 | U | 191-200 |
| | | 1858 | 1858-70 | V | 77-80 |
| | Baltimore | 1858 | 1858-70 | V | 77-82 |
| | | 1853 (2nd Sec.) | 1858-70 | V | 357-358 |

## Massachusetts

| | | | | | |
|---|---|---|---|---|---|
| Massachusetts | | 1818 | 1818-32 | B | 1-97 |
| | | 1818 | 1820-44 | C | 1-35 |
| | | 1818 | 1833-48 | D | 79-120 |
| | | 1832 | 1833-48 | E | 187-242 |
| | | 1832 | 1831-48 | G | 95-159 |
| | | 1832 | 1849-68 | I | 67-96 (found after page 62) |
| | | 1832 | 1831-48 | J | 274-278 |
| | | Invalid | 1843-57 | K | 55-68 |
| | | Invalid | 1855-66 | L-1 | 45-59 |
| | | 1818 | 1848-61 | M | 29-34 |
| | | 1828 | 1848-61 | M | 435-436 |
| | | 1853 (2nd Sec.) | 1853-61 | M | 189-198, 521-532 |
| | | 1836 | 1831-43 | N | 38-49, 141-143, 145-161 |
| | | 1836 | 1844-53 | O | 39-55 |
| | | 1838,1843,1844 | 1836-48 | P | 102-168 |
| | | 1848 | 1848-61 | R | 157-258 |
| | | 1836,1848 | 1862-70 | T | 7-8 |
| | | 1848 | 1862-70 | T | 107-112 |
| | | 1853 (2nd Sec.) | 1862-70 | T | 267-271 |
| | | 1853 (1st Sec.) | 1853-57 | U | 65-80 |
| | | 1858 | 1858-70 | V | 17-22 |
| | Boston | 1858 | 1858-70 | V | 17-24 |
| | | 1853 (2nd Sec.) | 1862-70 | T | 267-271 |

## Michigan Territory and Michigan

| | | | | | |
|---|---|---|---|---|---|
| Michigan | | 1818 | 1818-32 | B | 406-415 |
| | | 1818 | 1820-44 | C | 428-439 |
| | | 1818 | 1833-48 | D | 316-325 |
| | | 1832 | 1831-48 | G | 424-433 |
| | | 1832 | 1849-68 | I | 407-410 |

|  |  | 1832 | 1831-48 | J | 332 only |
|---|---|---|---|---|---|
|  |  | Invalid | 1843-57 | K | 355-361, 391-396 |
|  |  | Invalid | 1855-66 | L-2 | 219-235 |
|  |  | 1818 | 1848-61 | M | 115-116 |
|  |  | 1828 | 1848-61 | M | 509-510 |
|  |  | 1853 (2nd Sec.) | 1853-61 | M | 402-405 |
|  |  | 1836 | 1831-43 | N | 208-211 |
|  |  | 1836 | 1844-60 | O | 265-271 |
|  |  | 1838,1843,1844 | 1836-48 | Q | 361-364 |
|  |  | 1848 | 1848-61 | R | 329-332 |
|  |  | 1836,1848 | 1862-70 | T | 230 only |
|  |  | 1848 | 1862-70 | T | 55 only |
|  |  | 1853 (1st Sec.) | 1853-57 | U | 432-441 |
|  | Detroit | 1858 | 1858-70 | V | 261-265 |
|  |  | 1853 (2nd Sec.) | 1858-70 | V | 379-380 |
|  | Grand Rapids | 1848 | 1848-70 | T | 231 only |
|  |  | 1858 | 1858-70 | V | 266-268 |
|  |  | 1853 (2nd Sec.) | 1858-70 | V | 463-464 |

Minnesota

| Minnesota |  | Invalid | 1855-66 | L-2 | 275-280 |
|---|---|---|---|---|---|
|  |  | 1853 (2nd Sec.) | 1853-61 | M | 411 only (missing from microfilm) |
|  |  | 1848 | 1848-61 | R | 323-326 |
|  |  | 1836,1848 | 1862-70 | T | 60 only |
|  |  | 1848 | 1862-70 | T | 236 only |
|  |  | 1853 (1st Sec.) | 1853-57 | U | 458-461 |
|  | Fairfield | 1858 | 1858-70 | V | 340-342 |
|  | St. Paul | 1853 (2nd Sec.) | 1848-61 | M | 417 only |
|  |  | 1858 | 1858-70 | V | 282 only, 398-400 |

Mississippi

| Mississippi |  | 1818 | 1818-32 | B | 416-423 |
|---|---|---|---|---|---|
|  |  | 1818 | 1820-44 | C | 440-450 |
|  |  | 1818 | 1833-48 | E | 182-183 |
|  |  | 1832 | 1831-48 | G | 412-417 |

| | | | | | |
|---|---|---|---|---|---|
| | | 1832 | 1849-68 | I | 313-316 |
| | | 1832 | 1831-48 | J | 317 only |
| | | Invalid | 1843-57 | K | 255-258 |
| | | Invalid | 1855-66 | L-1 | 279-282 |
| | | 1818 | 1848-61 | M | 89-92 |
| | | 1828 | 1848-61 | M | 481-482 |
| | | 1853 (2nd Sec.) | 1853-61 | M | 355-356 |
| | | 1836 | 1831-43 | N | 12-37 |
| | | 1836 | 1844-60 | O | 205-208 |
| | | 1838,1843,1844 | 1836-48 | Q | 341-346 |
| | | 1848 | 1848-61 | R | 333-338 |
| | | 1836,1848 | 1862-70 | T | 14 only |
| | | 1848 | 1862-70 | T | 183-184 |
| | | 1853 (1st Sec.) | 1853-57 | U | 310-315 |
| | Jackson (changed to Vicksburg) | 1858 | 1858-70 | V | 131-134 |

Missouri

| | | | | | |
|---|---|---|---|---|---|
| Missouri | | 1818 | 1818-1832 | B | 395-405 |
| | | 1818 | 1820-44 | C | 417-427 |
| | | 1818 | 1833-48 | E | 180-181 |
| | | 1832 | 1831-48 | H | 394-402 |
| | | 1832 | 1849-68 | I | 427-430 |
| | | 1832 | 1831-48 | J | 331 only |
| | | Invalid | 1843-57 | K | 307-315, 375-380 |
| | | Invalid | 1855-66 | L-2 | 29-46 |
| | | 1818 | 1848-61 | M | 109-110 |
| | | 1828 | 1848-61 | M | 503-504 |
| | | 1853 (2nd Sec.) | 1853-61 | M | 385-386 |
| | | 1836 | 1831-43 | N | 218-219 |
| | | 1836 | 1844-53 | O | 241-244, 357-363 |
| | | 1838,1843,1844 | 1836-48 | Q | 327-334 |
| | | 1848 | 1848-61 | R | 339-344 |
| | | 1848 | 1862-70 | T | 205-207 |
| | | 1853 (1st Sec.) | 1853-57 | U | 398-409 |
| | | 1853 (2nd Sec.) | 1858-70 | V | 370 only |
| Macon City | | 1853 (2nd Sec.) | 1848-61 | M | 412 only (missing from microfilm) |

| | | 1853 (1st Sec.) | 1853-57 | U | 487 only |
|---|---|---|---|---|---|
| | | 1858 | 1858-70 | V | 252-254 |
| | | 1853 (2nd Sec.) | 1858-70 | V | 424 only |
| St. Louis | | 1836,1848 | 1862-70 | T | 44 only |
| | | 1858 | 1858-70 | V | 255-260 |

## Nebraska

| | | | | | |
|---|---|---|---|---|---|
| Nebraska | 1853 (2nd Sec.) | 1853-61 | | M | 413-414 |
| | 1848 | 1848-61 | | R | 345-348 |
| | 1853 (1st Sec.) | 1853-57 | | U | 462-463 |
| Omaha | 1853 (2nd Sec.) | 1858-70 | | V | 511 - end |

## New Mexico

| | | | | | |
|---|---|---|---|---|---|
| New Mexico | 1853 (1st Sec.) | 1853-61 | | U | 300-303 |
| Santa Fe | 1858 | 1858-70 | | V | 278 only |

## New Hampshire

| | | | | | |
|---|---|---|---|---|---|
| New Hampshire | 1818 | 1818-32 | | B | 239-290 |
| | 1818 | 1833-48 | | D | 47-78 |
| | 1818 | 1833-48 | | E | 241-266 |
| | 1832 | 1831-48 | | H | 169-222 |
| | 1828 | 1831-48 | | J | 278-280 |
| Concord | 1818 | 1820-44 | | C | 605-610 |
| | 1832 | 1833-48 | | F | 14-61 |
| | 1832 | 1849-68 | | I | 23-36 |
| | 1818 | 1831-48 | | J | 222-235 |
| | 1828 | 1831-48 | | J | 266-267 |
| | Invalid | 1843-57 | | K | 25-34 |
| | Invalid | 1855-66 | | L-1 | 24-30 |
| | 1818 | 1848-61 | | M | 13-18 |
| | 1828 | 1848-61 | | M | 429-430 |
| | 1853 (2nd Sec.) | 1853-61 | | M | 159-168 |
| | 1836 | 1831-43 | | N | 62-66, 196-197 |
| | 1836 | 1844-60 | | O | 17-23 |
| | 1838,1843,1844 | 1836-48 | | P | 66-101 |
| | 1848 | 1848-61 | | R | 349-388 |
| | 1848 | 1862-70 | | T | 93-97 |
| | 1836,1848 | 1862-70 | | T | 4 only |
| | 1853 (1st Sec.) | 1853-57 | | U | 30-40 |
| | 1858 | 1858-70 | | V | 8 only, 279-281 |

| | | | | |
|---|---|---|---|---|
| | 1853 (2nd Sec.) | 1862-70 | T | 260-261, 293-294 |
| Portsmouth | 1818 | 1818-32 | C | 365-381 |
| | 1832 | 1831-48 | H | 169-222 |
| | 1832 | 1849-68 | I | 19-22 |
| | Invalid | 1843-57 | K | 15-24 |
| | Invalid | 1855-66 | L-1 | 29-23 |
| | 1818 | 1848-61 | M | 9-12 |
| | 1828 | 1848-61 | M | 427-428 |
| | 1853 (2nd Sec.) | 1853-61 | M | 148-158 |
| | 1836 | 1831-43 | N | 57-61 |
| | 1836 | 1844-60 | O | 11-16 |
| | 1838,1843,1844 | 1836-48 | Q | 43-65 |
| | 1848 | 1848-61 | R | 389-406 |
| | 1836,1848 | 1862-70 | T | 3 only |
| | 1848 | 1862-70 | T | 89-92 |
| | 1853 (2nd Sec.) | 1862-70 | V | 259 only |
| | 1858 | 1858-70 | V | 5-7 |
| | 1853 (1st Sec.) | 1853-57 | U | 22-29 |

New Jersey

| | | | | |
|---|---|---|---|---|
| New Jersey | 1818 | 1818-32 | A | 588-631 |
| | 1818 | 1820-44 | C | 141-158 |
| | 1818 | 1833-48 | D | 448-468 |
| | 1818 | 1833-48 | E | 1-20 |
| | 1832 | 1831-48 | G | 208-233 |
| | 1832 | 1849-68 | I | 191-202 |
| | 1832 | 1831-48 | J | 300-301 |
| | Invalid | 1843-57 | K | 131-136 |
| | Invalid | 1855-66 | L-1 | 150-156 |
| | 1818 | 1848-61 | M | 55-56 |
| | 1828 | 1848-61 | M | 447-448 |
| | 1853 (2nd Sec.) | 1853-61 | M | 265-274 |
| | 1836 | 1831-43 | N | 108-113 |
| | 1836 | 1844-53 | O | 119-128 |
| | 1838,1843,1844 | 1836-48 | P | 346-367 |
| | 1848 | 1848-61 | R | 1-16 |
| | 1836,1848 | 1862-70 | T | 15 only |
| | 1848 | 1862-70 | T | 137-140 |
| | 1853 (1st Sec.) | 1853-57 | U | 155-164 |
| | 1853 (2nd Sec.) | 1862-70 | T | 289-291 |
| | 1858 | 1858-70 | V | 51-54 |

| New York | 1818 | 1818-32 | A | 62-210 |
|---|---|---|---|---|
| | 1818 | 1818-32 | A | 632-650 |
| | 1818 | 1820-44 | C | 497-512 |
| | 1818 | 1833-48 | D | 299-315 |
| | 1832 | 1849-68 | I | 179-190 |
| | 1832 | 1831-48 | J | 137-193 |
| | 1828 | 1831-48 | J | 286-289 |
| | Invalid | 1843-57 | K | 82-96, 381-390 |
| | Invalid | 1855-66 | L-1 | 124-149 |
| | 1818 | 1848-61 | M | 41-43 |
| | 1828 | 1848-61 | M | 441-442 |
| | 1853 (2nd Sec.) | 1853-61 | M | 225-240 |
| | 1836 | 1831-43 | N | 2-4, 98-103 |
| | 1836 | 1844-60 | O | 81-90, 368-381 |
| | 1838,1843,1848 | 1836-48 | Q | 316-345 |
| | 1848 | 1848-61 | S | 79-102 |
| | 1836,1848 | 1862-70 | T | 11-12 |
| | 1848 | 1862-70 | T | 123-126 |
| | 1853 (1st Sec.) | 1853-57 | U | 105-124 |
| | 1858 | 1858-70 | V | 43-50 |
| | 1853 (2nd Sec.) | 1858-70 | V | 278-279 |
| Albany | 1818 | 1820-44 | C | 66-113 |
| | 1818 | 1833-48 | D | 205-281 |
| | 1818 | 1833-48 | E | 268-317 |
| | 1832 | 1831-48 | G | 1-94 |
| | 1832 | 1849-68 | I | 129-178 |
| | 1832 | 1831-48 | J | 1-136 |
| | 1828 | 131-48 | J | 289-299 |
| | Invalid | 1843-57 | K | 97-130, 243 only |
| | Invalid | 1855-66 | L-1 | 71-123 |
| | 1818 | 1848-61 | M | 44-53 |
| | 1828 | 1848-61 | M | 443-445 |
| | 1853 (2nd Sec.) | 1853-61 | M | 241-264, 512-520 |
| | 1836 | 1831-43 | N | 7-11, 104-107, 178-191, 193-195 |
| | 1836 | 1844-60 | O | 91-118 |
| | 1838,1843,1844 | 1836-48 | P | 259-315,386-405 |
| | 1848 | 1848-61 | S | 17-78 |
| | 1848 | 1862-70 | T | 127-134 |

| | 1836,1848 | 1862-70 | T | 13-14 |
|---|---|---|---|---|
| | 1853 (1st Sec.) | 1853-57 | U | 125-149 |
| | 1858 | 1858-70 | V | 33-40 |
| | 1853 (2nd Sec.) | 1862-70 | T | 280-288, 292only |
| Brooklyn | 1858 | 1858-70 | V | 33-40 |
| | 1853 (2nd Sec.) | 1862-70 | V | 465-70 |
| | 1853 (1st Sec.) | 1858-57 | U | 485-486 |
| | 1836,1848 | 1862-70 | T | 63-64 |
| Buffalo | 1818 | 1818-32 | B | 490-510 |
| | 1818 | 1820-44 | C | 513-538 |
| | 1818 | 1833-48 | D | 299-315 |
| | 1832 | 1831-48 | G | 386-403 |
| Canandaigua | 1818 | 1848-61 | M | 54 only |
| | 1828 | 1848-61 | M | 446 only |
| | 1853 (2nd Sec.) | 1853-61 | M | 533-547 |
| | 1836 | 1831-43 | N | 122-123 |
| | 1836,1848 | 1862-70 | T | 71-80 |
| | 1853 (1st Sec.) | 1853-57 | U | 150-154 |
| | 1858 | 1858-70 | V | 321-335 |
| Utica | 1818 | 1818-32 | B | 511-530 |
| | 1818 | 1820-44 | C | 539-578 |
| | 1818 | 1833-48 | D | 282-298 |
| | 1832 | 1831-48 | G | 333-356 |

North Carolina

| North Carolina | 1818 | 1818-32 | B | 318-342 |
|---|---|---|---|---|
| | 1818 | 1820-44 | C | 249-266 |
| | 1818 | 1833-48 | E | 100-111 |
| | 1832 | 1833-48 | E | 318-347 |
| | 1832 | 1831-48 | H | 340-361 |
| | 1832 | 1849-68 | I | 263-276 |
| | 1818, 1828, 1832 | 1831-48 | J | 311-313 |
| | Invalid | 1843-57 | K | 209-213 |
| | 1818 | 1848-61 | M | 71-72 |
| | 1828 | 1848-61 | M | 463-464 |
| | 1836 | 1831-43 | N | 5-6, 130-131, 140 only |
| | 1836 | 1844-53 | O | 173-181, 383-385 |
| | 1838,1843,1844 | 1836-48 | Q | 103-130 |
| | 1848 | 1848-61 | S | 103-120 |

| Ashville | 1832 | 1849-68 | I | 441-445 |
|---|---|---|---|---|
|  | Invalid | 1843-57 | K | 455-458 |
|  | 1818 | 1848-61 | M | 125 only |
|  | 1853 (2nd Sec.) | 1853-61 | M | 323-324 |
|  | 1836 | 1844-53 | O | 453-454 |
|  | 1838,1843,1844 | 1836-48 | Q | 376-377 |
|  | 1848 | 1848-61 | S | 121-126 |
|  | 1853 (1st Sec.) | 1853-57 | U | 240-245 |
| Ashville (changed to Raleigh) | 1858 | 1858-70 | V | 107-112 |
| Morgantown | Invalid | 1855-66 | L-1 | 244-248 |
|  | 1836 | 1844-53 | O | 453-454 |
|  | 1848 | 1862-70 | T | 167-170 |
|  | 1858 | 1858-70 | V | 113-114 |
| Raleigh | 1853 (2nd Sec.) | 1858-70 | V | 493-496 |

Ohio

| Ohio | 1818 | 1818-32 | A | 468-516 |
|---|---|---|---|---|
|  | 1818 | 1820-44 | C | 351-364 |
|  | 1818 | 1833-48 | E | 152-169 |
|  | 1832 | 1833-48 | F | 135-157 |
|  | 1832 | 1831-48 | H | 286-319 |
|  | 1832 | 1849-68 | I | 395-406 |
|  | 1818, 1828, 1832 | 1831-48 | J | 324-326 |
|  | Invalid | 1843-57 | K | 365-370 |
|  | 1818 | 1848-61 | M | 117-120 |
|  | 1828 | 1848-61 | M | 499 only |
|  | 1836 | 1831-43 | N | 132-133 |
|  | 1836 | 1844-53 | O | 261-264, 387-394 |
|  | 1838,1843,1844 | 1836-48 | Q | 273-298 |
|  | 1848 | 1848-61 | S | 127-136 |
|  | 1836,1848 | 1862-70 | T | 53 only |
| Cincinnati | Invalid | 1843-57 | K | 344-354, 418 only |
|  | Invalid | 1855-66 | L-2 | 111-131 |
|  | 1853 (2nd Sec.) | 1853-61 | M | 387-396 |
|  | 1836,1848 | 1862-70 | T | 51-52 |
|  | 1848 | 1862-70 | T | 221-224 |
|  | 1853 (1st Sec.) | 1853-57 | U | 410-424 |
|  | 1858 | 1858-70 | V | 175-182 |
|  | 1853 (2nd Sec.) | 1858-70 | V | 372-375 |

| Cleveland | 1832 | 1849-68 | I | 433-438 |
|---|---|---|---|---|
| | Invalid | 1843-57 | K | 459-466 |
| | Invalid | 1855-66 | L-2 | 132-146 |
| | 1818 | 1848-61 | M | 121-124 |
| | 1828 | 1848-61 | M | 511 only |
| | 1853 (2nd Sec.) | 1853-61 | M | 397-402 |
| | 1836 | 1831-43 | N | 455-460 |
| | 1838,1843,1844 | 1836-48 | Q | 372-375 |
| | 1848 | 1848-61 | S | 321-328 |
| | 1848 | 1862-70 | T | 226-229 |
| | 1836,1848 | 1862-70 | T | 53 only |
| | 1853 (1st Sec.) | 1853-57 | U | 425-431, 463 only |
| | 1858 | 1858-70 | V | 185-190 |
| | 1853 (2nd Sec.) | 1858-70 | V | 376-378 |
| Columbus | 1836,1848 | 1862-70 | T | 54 only |
| | 1848 | 1862-70 | T | 225 only |
| | 1858 | 1858-70 | V | 336-339 |
| | 1853 (2nd Sec.) | 1858-70 | V | 387-92 |
| | 1853 (1st Sec.) | 1853-57 | U | 467-469 |

Oregon

| Oregon | Invalid | 1843-57 | K | 471-474 |
|---|---|---|---|---|
| | Invalid | 1855-66 | L-2 | 256-259 |
| | 1853 (2nd Sec.) | 1853-61 | M | 351 only |
| | 1836 | 1844-53 | O | 402 only |
| Oregon City | 1836 | 1844-53 | O | 466 only |
| | 1836,1848 | 1862-70 | T | 56 only |
| | 1848 | 1862-70 | T | 232 only |
| | 1853 (1st Sec.) | 1853-57 | U | 297-299, 489 only |
| Oregon and Oregon City | 1858 | 1858-70 | V | 221-222 |

Pennsylvania

| Pennsylvania | 1818 | 1818-32 | A | 211-290 |
|---|---|---|---|---|
| | 1832 | 1833-48 | D | 469-481 |
| | 1818 | 1833-48 | E | 21-44 |
| | 1832 | 1831-48 | G | 234-273 |
| | 1832 | 1849-68 | I | 203-218 |
| | 1836 | 1831-48 | J | 263 only |
| | 1828 | 1831-48 | J | 302-304 |
| | Invalid | 1843-57 | K | 136-156 |

| | 1836 | 1831-43 | N | 114-117, 229-230 |
|---|---|---|---|---|
| Philadelphia | 1818 | 1820-44 | C | 159-188 |
| | 1828 | 1831-48 | J | 302-305 |
| | Invalid | 1843-57 | K | 181 only |
| | Invalid | 1855-66 | L-1 | 157-180 |
| | 1818 | 1848-61 | M | 57-58 |
| | 1828 | 1848-61 | M | 449-450 |
| | 1853 (2nd Sec.) | 1853-61 | M | 275-284 |
| | 1836 | 1844-53 | O | 129-140, 273 only, 278-284 |
| | 1838,1843,1844 | 1836-48 | Q | 2-28 |
| | 1848 | 1848-61 | S | 137-164 |
| | 1836,1848 | 1862-70 | T | 16-17 |
| | 1848 | 1862-70 | T | 141-144 |
| | 1853 (1st Sec.) | 1853-57 | U | 165-176 |
| | 1858 | 1858-70 | V | 55-64 |
| | 1853 (2nd Sec.) | 1858-70 | V | 350-353 |
| Pittsburg | 1818 | 1818-32 | B | 462-489 |
| | 1818 | 1820-44 | C | 475-496 |
| | 1818 | 1833-48 | E | 45-62 |
| | 1832 | 1833-48 | E | 377-401 |
| | 1832 | 1831-48 | G | 274-296 |
| | 1832 | 1849-68 | I | 219-230 |
| | 1828 | 1831-48 | J | 327-329 |
| | Invalid | 1843-57 | K | 157-170 |
| | Invalid | 1855-66 | L-1 | 181-198 |
| | 1818 | 1848-61 | M | 59-62 |
| | 1828 | 1848-61 | M | 451-454 |
| | 1853 (2nd Sec.) | 1853-61 | M | 285-290 |
| | 1836 | 1831-43 | N | 124-125 |
| | 1836 | 1844-53 | O | 141-148 |
| | 1838,1843,1844 | 1836-48 | Q | 29-47 |
| | 1848 | 1848-61 | S | 165-178 |
| | 1836,1848 | 1862-70 | T | 18 only |
| | 1848 | 1862-70 | T | 145-148 |
| | 1853 (1st Sec.) | 1853-57 | U | 177-190 |
| | 1858 | 1858-70 | V | 71-74, |
| | 1853 (2nd Sec.) | 1858-70 | V | 354-356 |

## Rhode Island

| Rhode Island | 1818 | 1818-32 | B | 291-317 |
|---|---|---|---|---|
| | 1818 | 1820-44 | C | 114-123 |
| | 1818 | 1833-48 | D | 121-138 |

| | | | | |
|---|---|---|---|---|
| | 1832 | 1833-48 | D | 430-447 |
| | 1832 | 1831-48 | H | 140-168 |
| | 1832 | 1849-68 | I | 119-128 |
| | 1832 | 1831-48 | J | 333 only |
| | 1818, 1828, 1832 | 1831-48 | J | 280 only |
| | Invalid | 1843-57 | K | 69-72 |
| | Invalid | 1855-66 | L-1 | 60-63 |
| | 1818 | 1848-61 | M | 35-36 |
| | 1828 | 1848-61 | M | 437-438 |
| | 1853 (2nd Sec.) | 1853-61 | N | 215-224 |
| | 1836 | 1831-43 | N | 88-97, 168 only |
| | 1836 | 1844-53 | O | 55-64 |
| | 1838,1843,1844 | 1836-48 | P | 196-214 |
| | 1848 | 1848-61 | S | 179-194 |
| | 1836,1848 | 1862-70 | T | 9 only |
| | 1848 | 1862-70 | T | 113-116 |
| | 1853 (1st Sec.) | 1853-57 | U | 96-104 |
| | 1853 (2nd Sec.) | 1862-70 | T | 276-277 |
| Providence | 1858 | 1858-70 | V | 25-28 |

South Carolina

| | | | | |
|---|---|---|---|---|
| South Carolina | 1818 | 1818-32 | B | 343-360 |
| | 1818 | 1820-44 | C | 267-286 |
| | 1818 | 1833-48 | E | 112-116 |
| | 1832 | 1833-48 | F | 180 only |
| | 1832 | 1831-48 | H | 362-379 |
| | 1832 | 1849-68 | I | 277-282 |
| | 1818, 1828, 1832 | 1831-48 | J | 313-314 |
| | Invalid | 1843-57 | K | 214-219 |
| | Invalid | 1855-66 | L-1 | 249-255 |
| | 1818 | 1848-61 | M | 73-74 |
| | 1828 | 1848-61 | M | 465-466 |
| | 1853 (2nd Sec.) | 1853-61 | M | 325-328 |
| | 1836 | 1831-43 | N | 136-137, 144 only |
| | 1836 | 1844-55 | O | 182-187 |
| | 1838,1843,1844 | 1836-48 | Q | 131-148 |
| | 1848 | 1848-61 | S | 195-202 |
| | 1836,1848 | 1862-70 | T | 26 only |
| | 1848 | 1862-70 | T | 171-173 |

| | 1853 (1st Sec.) | 1853-57 | U | 246-255 |
|---|---|---|---|---|
| Charleston | 1858 | 1858-70 | V | 117-120 |

Tennessee

| | | | | |
|---|---|---|---|---|
| East (Knoxville) | 1818 | 1818-32 | A | 517-553 |
| | 1818 | 1820-44 | C | 344-350 |
| | 1818 | 1833-48 | D | 384-403 |
| | 1818 | 1833-48 | E | 124-128 |
| | 1832 | 1831-48 | H | 255-268 |
| West | 1818 | 1818-32 | A | 554-587 |
| | 1818 | 1820-44 | C | 329-343 |
| | 1832 | 1833-48 | D | 359-383 |
| | 1818 | 1833-48 | E | 129-133 |
| | 1832 | 1831-48 | H | 269-285 |
| | 1836 | 1836-43 | N | 138-139 |
| Jackson | 1818 | 1820-44 | C | 585-590 |
| | 1832 | 1831-48 | G | 441-443,447-459 |
| | 1832 | 1849-68 | I | 321-326 |
| | 1818,1828,1832 | 1831-48 | J | 204-207, 319 only |
| | Invalid | 1843-57 | K | 285-288 |
| | Invalid | 1855-66 | L-2 | 88-91 |
| | 1818 | 1848-61 | M | 101-102 |
| | 1828 | 1848-61 | M | 493-494 |
| | 1853 (2nd Sec.) | 1853-61 | M | 359-360 |
| | 1836 | 1853-61 | O | 226-228 |
| | 1838,1843,1844 | 1836-48 | Q | 220-228 |
| | 1848 | 1848-61 | S | 203-206 |
| | 1836,1848 | 1862-70 | T | 41 only |
| | 1848 | 1862-70 | T | 198-199 |
| | 1853 (1st Sec.) | 1853-57 | U | 320-323 |
| | 1858 | 1858-70 | V | 217-220 |
| Jonesboro | 1818 | 1820-44 | C | 595-596 |
| | 1818 | 1833-48 | E | 186 only |
| | 1832 | 1831-48 | H | 438-459 |
| | 1832 | 1849-68 | I | 351-356 |
| | 1818,1828,1832 | 1831-48 | J | 320 only |
| | Invalid | 1843-57 | K | 262-266, 364 only, 404-407 |
| | Invalid | 1855-66 | L-2 | 73-87 |
| | 1818 | 1848-61 | M | 93-94 |
| | 1828 | 1848-61 | M | 485-486 |

| | | | | |
|---|---|---|---|---|
| | 1853 (2nd Sec.) | 1853-61 | M | 369-370 |
| | 1836 | 1836-43 | N | 136 only |
| | 1836 | 1844-53 | O | 212-216 |
| | 1838,1843,1844 | 1836-48 | Q | 199-205 |
| | 1848 | 1848-61 | S | 207-210 |
| | 1836,1848 | 1862-70 | T | 36 only |
| | 1848 | 1862-70 | T | 187-188 |
| | 1853 (1st Sec.) | 1853-57 | U | 342-346 |
| | 1858 | 1858-70 | V | 211-214 |
| Knoxville | 1832 | 1849-68 | I | 341-350 |
| | 1818, 1828, 1832 | 1831-48 | J | 320 only |
| | Invalid | 1843-57 | K | 267-273, 408-410 |
| | Invalid | 1855-66 | L-2 | 60-72 |
| | 1818 | 1848-61 | M | 95-96 |
| | 1828 | 1848-61 | M | 487-488 |
| | 1853 (2nd Sec.) | 1853-61 | M | 365-368 |
| | 1836 | 1831-43 | N | 224-225 |
| | 1836 | 1844-60 | O | 217-220, 228 only, 445-448 |
| | 1838,1843,1844 | 1836-50 | Q | 211-219 |
| | 1848 | 1848-61 | S | 211-216 |
| | 1836,1848 | 1862-70 | T | 37-38 |
| | 1848 | 1862-70 | T | 191-194 |
| | 1853 (1st Sec.) | 1853-57 | U | 334-341, 347 only |
| | 1858 | 1858-70 | V | 193-198 |
| | 1853 (2nd Sec.) | 1858-70 | V | 437-442 |
| Nashville | 1832 | 1849-68 | I | 331-340 |
| | 1818, 1828, 1832 | 1831-48 | J | 318-319 |
| | Invalid | 1843-57 | K | 274-284 |
| | Invalid | 1855-66 | L-2 | 47-59 |
| | 1818 | 1848-61 | M | 97-98 |
| | 1828 | 1848-61 | M | 489-490 |
| | 1853 (2nd Sec.) | 1853-61 | M | 361-364 |
| | 1836, 1843,1844 | 1836-48 | O | 221-225, 449-452 |
| | 1838,1843,1844 | 1836-48 | Q | 182b-198 |
| | 1848 | 1848-61 | S | 217-224 |
| | 1836,1848 | 1862-70 | T | 39-40 |
| | 1848 | 1862-70 | T | 195-197 |
| | 1853 (1st Sec.) | 1853-57 | U | 324-333 |
| | 1858 | 1858-70 | V | 203-208 |

| | 1853 (2nd Sec.) | 1858-70 | V | 477-480 |
|---|---|---|---|---|
| Pulaski | 1818 | 1820-44 | C | 602-603 |
| | 1832 | 1831-48 | G | 460-465 |
| | 1832 | 1849-68 | I | 327-330 |
| | 1818, 1828, 1832 | 1831-48 | J | 212-214, 334 only |
| | Invalid | 1843-57 | K | 289-290 |
| | 1818 | 1848-61 | M | 99-100 |
| | 1828 | 1848-61 | M | 491-492 |
| | 1853 (2nd Sec.) | 1853-61 | M | 357-358 |
| | 1836 | 1844-53 | O | 229-232 |
| | 1838,1843,1844 | 1836-48 | Q | 206-210 |
| | 1848 | 1848-61 | S | 225-228 |
| | 1853 (1st Sec.) | 1853-57 | U | 316-19 |

Texas

| | 1848 | 1862-70 | T | 237 only |
|---|---|---|---|---|
| | 1853 (1st Sec.) | 1853-57 | U | 294-95 |

Vermont

| Vermont | 1818 | 1818-32 | A | 1-62 |
|---|---|---|---|---|
| | 1832 | 1831-48 | G | 160-207 |
| | 1818 | 1831-48 | J | 238-253 |
| | 1828 | 1831-48 | J | 264-265, 284-286 |
| | 1838, 1848, 1843 | 1836-48 | P | 170-195 |
| | 1818 | 1820-44 | O | 611-616 |
| Bellows Falls | 1836 | 831-43 | M | 67-71 |
| Bradford (changed to St. Johnsburg) | Invalid | 1855-66 | L-1 | 31-38 |
| | 1853 (2nd Sec.) | 1848-61 | M | 179-188 |
| | 1836 | 1844-53 | O | 25-32 |
| | 1848 | 1848-63 | S | 229-264 |
| Burlington | 1818 | 1820-44 | C | 124-140 |
| | 1818 | 1833-48 | D | 169-204 |
| | 1832 | 1833-48 | D | 404-427 |
| | 1832 | 1831-48 | G | 160-207 |
| | Invalid | 1843-57 | K | 43-54 |
| (changed to Rutland) | Invalid | 1855-66 | L-1 | 39-44 |

| | | | | |
|---|---|---|---|---|
| | 1818 | 1848-61 | M | 25-28 |
| | 1828 | 1848-61 | M | 433 only |
| | 1853 (2nd Sec.) | 1848-61 | M | 169-178 |
| | 1836 | 1831-43 | N | 72-75 |
| | 1836 | 1844-53 | O | 33-38 |
| | 1838,1843,1844 | 1836-48 | P | 368-384 |
| | 1848 | 1848-61 | S | 265-278 |
| | 1853 (1st Sec.) | 1853-57 | U | 41-48 |
| Montpelier | 1832 | 1849-68 | I | 37-52 |
| | 1853 (2nd Sec.) | 1848-61 | K | 35-42 |
| | 1836 | 1831-43 | M | 67 only |
| | 1836 | 1844-53 | O | 24-32 |
| | 1838,1843,1844 | 1836-48 | P | 169-195, 383 only |
| (changed to Bradford) | 1853 (1st Sec.) | 1853-57 | U | 49-64 |
| Poultney | 1832 | 1849-68 | I | 53-66 |
| | 1853 (2nd Sec.) | 1848-61 | M | 69-178 |
| | 1848 | 1848-61 | S | 265-278 |
| (changed to Burlington) | 1836, 1848 | 1862-70 | T | 6 only |
| | 1848 | 1862-70 | T | 103-106 |
| (changed to Burlington) | 1858 | 1858-70 | V | 13-16 |
| | 1853 (2nd Sec.) | 1862-70 | T | 262-263 |
| St. Johnsbury | 1853 (2nd Sec.) | 1848-61 | M | 179-188 |
| | 1848 | 1848-63 | S | 229-264 |
| | 1848 | 1862-70 | T | 98-100 |
| (changed to Montpelier | 1836,1848 | 1862-70 | T | 5 only |
| | 1853 (1st Sec.) | 1853-57 | U | 49-64 |
| (changed to Montpelier) | 1858 | 1858-70 | V | 9-12 |
| | 1853 (2nd Sec.) | 1862-70 | T | 264-266 |
| Windsor or Bellows Falls | 1818 | 1820-44 | C | 611-616 |
| (Montpelier) | 1832 | 1833-48 | F | 62-105 |
| Windsor | 1818 | 1831-48 | J | 238-253 |
| | 1836 | 1831-43 | N | 67 only |
| | 1828 | 1831-48 | J | 264-265 |

## Virginia

| | | | | |
|---|---|---|---|---|
| Virginia | 1818 | 1818-32 | A | 366-423 |
| | 1818 | 1833-48 | E | 72-99 |

| | | | | |
|---|---|---|---|---|
| | 1832 | 1833-48 | E | 348-376 |
| | 1832 | 1833-48 | F | 106-127 |
| | 1832 | 1831-48 | G | 297-332 |
| | 1818, 1828, 1832 | 1831-48 | J | 307-311 |
| | Invalid | 1843-57 | K | 193-202 |
| | 1836 | 1831-43 | N | 120-121 |
| | 1836 | 1844-53 | O | 153-164 |
| | 1838,1843,1844 | 1836-48 | Q | 64-96 |
| Richmond | 1832 | 1849-68 | I | 23-256 |
| | Invalid | 1855-66 | L-1 | 226-234 |
| | 1818 | 1848-61 | M | 67-68 |
| | 1828 | 1848-61 | M | 459-460 |
| | 1853 (2$^{nd}$ Sec.) | 1848-61 | M | 297-307 |
| | 1848 | 1848-61 | S | 279-312 |
| | 1836,1848 | 1862-70 | T | 22 only |
| | 1848 | 1862-70 | T | 155-158 |
| | 1853 (1$^{st}$ Sec.) | 1853-57 | U | 214-225 |
| | 1858 | 1858-70 | V | 91-97 |
| | 1853 (2$^{nd}$ Sec.) | 1858-70 | V | 429-435 |
| Wheeling | 1818 | 1820-44 | C | 225-248 |
| | 1832 | 1833-48 | F | 1-13 |
| | 1832 | 1849-68 | I | 257-262 |
| | 1818 | 1831-1848 | J | 215-221 |
| | 1828 | 1831-48 | J | 268-269 |
| | Invalid | 1843-57 | K | 202-208 |
| | Invalid | 1855-66 | L-1 | 235-239 |
| | 1818 | 1848-61 | M | 69-70 |
| | 1828 | 1848-61 | M | 461-462 |
| | 1853 (2$^{nd}$ Sec.) | 18548-61 | M | 308-310 |
| | 1836 | 1831-43 | N | 194-195, 192 only, 198-207 |
| | 1836 | 1844-60 | O | 153-162 |
| | 1838,1843,1844 | 1836-48 | Q | 97-102 |
| | 1848 | 1848-61 | S | 313-316 |
| | 1848 | 1862-70 | T | 159-162 |
| | 1853 (1$^{st}$ Sec.) | 1853-57 | U | 226-229 |
| | 1858 | 1858-70 | V | 103-106 |
| | 1853 (2$^{nd}$ Sec.) | 1858-70 | V | 359-360 |

Wisconsin

| | | | | |
|---|---|---|---|---|
| Wisconsin | 1818 | 1820-44 | C | 597-601 |
| | 1832 | 1833-48 | F | 158-162 |
| | 1832 | 1849-68 | I | 411-422 |

| | 1818, 1828, 1832 | 1831-48 | J | 254-256 |
|---|---|---|---|---|
| | Invalid | 1843-57 | K | 320-324 |
| | Invalid | 1855-66 | L-2 | 236-243 |
| | 1818 | 1848-61 | M | 113-114 |
| | 1828 | 1848-61 | M | 507-508 |
| | 1853 (2nd Sec.) | 1853-61 | M | 407-408 |
| | 1836 | 1831-43 | N | 223 only |
| | 1836 | 1844-60 | O | 247-252 |
| | 1838,1843,1844 | 1836-48 | Q | 365-367 |
| | 1848 | 1848-61 | S | 317-320 |
| | 1848 | 1862-70 | T | 210-212 |
| | 1836, 1848 | 1862-70 | T | 46 only |
| | 1853 (1st Sec.) | 1853-57 | U | 442-449 |
| Madison | 1858 | 1858-70 | V | 276-277 |
| | 1853 (2nd Sec.) | 1858-70 | V | 386 only |
| Milwaukee | 1836,1848 | 1862-70 | T | 46 only |
| | 1858 | 1858-70 | V | 273-275 |
| | 1853 (2nd Sec.) | 1858-70 | V | 381 only |
| La Crosse | 1853 (2nd Sec.) | 1858-70 | V | 396-397 |

Washington Territory

| Washington Territory | Invalid | 1855-66 | L-2 | 261-268 |
|---|---|---|---|---|
| | 1848 | 1862-70 | T | 234 only |

* 9 7 8 0 7 8 8 4 5 5 8 6 5 *